Handmade
SURPRISES TOUCH HEARTS AND MAKE MEMORIES

From whimsical elves made of felt to clever greeting cards crafted at home, the inspired ideas in the all-new *Taste of Home Handmade Christmas* promise to make everyone's holiday merry and bright.

Whether you're new to crafting or a longtime pro, you'll enjoy projects such as Magnolia Leaf Wreath, Memory Wire Bracelets and so many others. These are the crafts you'll enjoy creating for family, friends, neighbors, teachers—everyone on your Christmas list.

Turn the page and you'll discover:

- **83 crafts** simply perfect for holiday gift-giving

- Dozens of **hints and tips** to customize your crafts and save time

- Clear step-by-step **directions** and **materials lists** of readily available items

- **Recycling projects** and ideas that use up scraps from your craft room

Decorate your home with Dried Fruit Garland, Pine Pomanders and Ice Candles. Liven up gift exchanges with Paper Ornament Gift Tags, Scrappy Ribbon Flowers and Holiday Wine Bottle Labels. And delight children with Cute Little Sock Critters and a Barn Animal Puppet Set. This year, add a bit of magic to everyone's holiday. It's easy with the heartfelt crafts you'll find only inside *Taste of Home Handmade Christmas*. Happy holidays!

11

33

TASTE OF HOME BOOKS • RDA ENTHUSIAST BRANDS, LLC • MILWAUKEE, WI

© 2019 RDA Enthusiast Brands, LLC.
1610 N. 2nd St., Suite 102
Milwaukee WI 53212-3906

Visit us at **tasteofhome.com** for other
Taste of Home books and products.
ISBN: 978-1-61765-864-8
LOCC: 2019934827

Deputy Editor: Mark Hagen
Senior Art Director: Raeann Thompson
Senior Designer: Courtney Lovetere
Designer: Jazmin Delgado
Copy Editor: Ann Walter

Pictured on front cover:
Rustic Christmas Tree, p. 6

Cover Photographer: Jim Wieland
Cover Set Stylist: Melissa Franco

**Pictured on back cover
(clockwise from top left):**
Chunky Silver Bracelet, p. 76; Decoupaged
Silhouette Plates, p. 30; Recycled Sweater Coffee
Sleeves, p. 61; Button Cards, p. 91; Whimsical
Woolen Elf, p. 22; Wooden Photo Ornaments,
p.17; Holiday Wine Bottle Labels, p. 95; Reindeer
Games, p. 19

Printed in China.
1 3 5 7 9 10 8 6 4 2

14

10

71

CONTENTS

48

More ways to connect with us:

Christmas
GONE RUSTIC

RUSTIC CHRISTMAS TREE

Ask the kids to gather sticks and twigs from the yard for this earthy yet simply whimsical decoration.

FINISHED SIZE

Wall hanging measures 13 in. tall by 9 in. wide, approximately.

MATERIALS

13x9-in. rectangular piece of barnwood or rustic wood for background
White acrylic craft paint
Wood stain
Small star-shaped wood cutouts in a variety of sizes
Variety of thin natural tree branches and twigs
Glue gun
Handsaw or hand pruners
White snowflake novelty buttons
Sawtooth hanger, optional

DIRECTIONS

1. Wipe the rectangular barnwood background piece clean. Mix 1 part white paint with 1 part water and brush over background piece. Wipe paint with cloth, creating an aged look. Let dry.
2. Following stain manufacturer's instructions, apply stain to desired wood stars. Let dry.
3. From a branch or twig, cut a piece measuring about 7 in. long for the widest part of tree. Cut about 22 more pieces, cutting each piece shorter than the last; Lay out the pieces in a tree pattern.
4. Cut two 2¼-in. pieces for the tree trunk. Cut one 2-in. piece and four 1-in. pieces for the tree topper.
5. Glue cut branch and twig pieces to the painted wood background piece in the planned Christmas tree shape. Let dry.
6. Glue snowflake buttons and wood star shapes to the tree and background where desired. Let dry.
7. Add sawtooth hanger to the back of piece for hanging if desired.

MAGNOLIA LEAF WREATH

It's easy to make a lovely holiday wreath with translucent, feathery leaves. Enjoy a rewarding afternoon, creating enough layers for a full effect.

FINISHED SIZE

Wreath measures about 16½ in. across.

MATERIALS

12-in. foam wreath form
About 200 magnolia skeleton leaves
¼ yd. natural burlap, cut into 2-in. strips
3-in. length of ¼-in. or 2-in. ribbon
2 straight pins
Glue gun
Decoupage glue
Fine white glitter
Foam stencil brush

DIRECTIONS

1. Cover work surface with waxed paper. Use brush to daub 5 leaves with the decoupage glue. On a clean sheet of waxed paper, pour glitter over leaves. Shake off excess glitter; let dry.
2. Wrap wreath form tightly with burlap strips, using glue gun to secure.
3. Using glue gun to glue 2 leaves at a time and placing leaf tips to the left, glue stalks of plain leaves to the form's inner rim. Moving toward the outer rim, glue 3 more pairs about 1 in. apart at stalks. Add another row of leaves about 2 in. to the right of first row. Continue adding rows, moving counterclockwise around form. Repeat once.
4. Add single leaves to fill in wreath as desired. If leaves become bent, gently reshape with your fingertips.
5. With glue gun, glue stems of glitter leaves to wreath as desired.
6. Loop ribbon for hanger; attach ends to back of wreath with glue gun and pins.

• • •

STICKS AND CONES

Choose one of three do-it-yourself scents for this dramatic centerpiece that's ideal for your seasonal table.

MATERIALS
Pine cones
Birch or other branches
Wide-mouthed glass jar
Ribbon
Essential oils for scented spray
** (recipes below)**
Unscented witch hazel
Distilled water
Plastic spray bottle
Plastic funnel (do not reuse for food)

Apple Pie Spice Scented Spray
** 10 drops cinnamon essential oil**
** 5 drops clove essential oil**

Orange Spice Scented Spray
** 10 drops orange essential oil**
** 5 drops cinnamon essential oil**

Winter Essence Scented Spray
** 10 drops pine essential oil**
** 5 drops peppermint essential oil**

DIRECTIONS
1. Select one of the three scented sprays. Insert funnel into top of open spray bottle. Pour in 2 Tbsp. unscented witch hazel and 6 Tbsp. distilled water. Add drops of the essential oils according to the chosen scent. Place the spray cap back on bottle. Shake gently until oils are mixed well.
2. Gather pine cones and cut branches from outdoors or purchase these items from a craft store. Lay the pine cones on a flat, cleanable surface. Mist pine cones all over with scented spray and let dry. Place scented pine cones in glass jar, filling to brim.
3. Arrange the cut ends of branches among the pine cones. Wrap a length of ribbon around center of jar, knot in place and trim ends.

UPCYCLED DOILY RUNNER

Stitched together, doilies from thrift or dollar stores—or your old linen drawer!—make an elegant and eye-catching runner. Keep it pristine white, or throw in dashes of color in holiday-appropriate shades. Substitute lace doilies for even more variation.

MATERIALS
Several crocheted or
** knit cotton doilies**
Sewing pins
Needle and thread
Household iron

DIRECTIONS
1. Iron all the doilies flat and arrange them in a long, roughly rectangular runner shape.
2. Use sewing pins to secure the doilies.
3. Use a needle and a coordinating colored thread to stitch the doilies together one at a time where their edges meet.
4. Remove the sewing pins; if needed, iron the runner flat.

STENCILED PEACE SIGN

Stand this sign of the season next to your front door for a meaningful greeting. Rub through the red paint layer with sandpaper for a one-of-a-kind rustic look.

FINISHED SIZE
Varies.

MATERIALS
New or repurposed wood plank
Latex paint—red for main color, yellow for contrasting color, antique white for lettering
Letter stencils of choice to spell "PEACE"
Painter's tape
2 bristle paintbrushes
Foam paintbrush
Sandpaper

DIRECTIONS
1. If necessary, clean the wood plank by wiping with a damp cloth; let dry.
2. Using broad strokes and following the wood grain, generously apply 1 coat of contrasting-color paint to plank with bristle paintbrush. Let dry. Apply a second coat in the same way and let dry.
3. Apply 2-3 coats of the main-color paint the same as before, letting each coat dry before applying the next coat.
4. When the plank is completely dry, place letter stencils in center of plank to spell "PEACE" and tape in place.
5. Using the foam brush, daub the lettering-color paint along the stencils. Let dry. Apply a second coat and let dry completely. Remove stencils.
6. Create a distressed look by lightly sanding the corners and edges of sign, following the wood grain and applying more or less pressure as needed to reveal desired amount of undercoat. Sand lightly over letters.

HOMEMADE HELPER
If your wood plank has knots or other character traits, highlight them by sanding those areas more vigorously.

ROPE THEM IN

Twist it, tie it and welcome guests to your home for the holidays.

FINISHED SIZE
Wreath measures about 16 in. across.

MATERIALS
62 ft. of ½-in.-wide sisal twisted rope
14-in.-wide wire wreath frame
22-gauge floral wire
Choice of decorations such as
florals and greenery
Utility knife
Wire cutters
Hot glue gun

DIRECTIONS
1. Use utility knife to cut four 1-yd. lengths of rope; set rope aside for Step 4.
2. Place wire wreath frame flat to work. Layer most of the remaining 50 ft. of rope in circular loops on top of frame.
3. With about 6 ft. of remaining rope, create a double hanging loop at top of wreath. Wrap remainder of rope tightly around itself and the wire frame backing. Secure hanging loop to back side with a clove hitch or simple knot. Apply hot glue to end of rope and knot to secure in place and prevent fraying.
4. In 4 symmetrically placed points on the wreath, wrap 1 of the remaining 1-yd. pieces tightly around the ropes and wire frame (see photo as a guide.) Secure each wrapped piece in place with a knot on the back side of the wreath. Use hot glue to prevent fraying.
5. Use wire cutters to cut several segments of floral wire. Attach layered strands of rope to wire frame using floral wire segments. Secure in at least 6 places around back side of the frame, making sure the rope does not sag.
6. Use hot glue to attach decorations such as silk flowers, mistletoe, or freshly cut evergreen or holly branches.

> **HOMEMADE HELPER**
> This weight of rope is easy to work with, but may sag if not fastened well to a strong wire wreath frame.

TINY TREES

Pine cones mimic their parent conifers in these tabletop designs. What a fun, easy way to bring a bit of the outdoors inside this season.

MATERIALS

Pine cones
Green spray paint
Various pots or votive candleholders
Decorative stars for tree toppers
Spray paint for stars, if desired
Tissue paper
Hot glue gun

DIRECTIONS

1. Spray-paint pine cones with green paint. Dry completely.
2. Fill pots or candleholders with crumpled tissue paper.
3. Gently insert pine cone trees into the bases and adhere to the tissue paper with hot glue.
4. Spray-paint decorative stars if desired. Allow to dry completely and adhere to the top of the pine cones with hot glue.

2. Starting at the bottom of the cage, begin bunching fresh greens and tying them into place with twine. Work upward in a circle, adding greens as needed to cover the cage. Trim any stems at the top and tuck the twine out of sight. Arrange the greens and trim with hand pruners. Mist the whole tree well with water to keep it fresh.

3. Rinse and drain cranberries. Cut a 6-ft. length of strong thread and tie a large knot at one end. Thread the other end onto a needle. Alternate cranberries with three kernels of unsalted, unbuttered popcorn (plain microwaved popcorn is fine) on the thread until filled; tie a knot to finish. Tie one end of the garland to a wire spoke at the top of the tree. Wrap the garland around the tree and tie the other end to the cage or a strong branch.

4. Tie a piece of baker's twine to the top of each of several pine cones. Spread peanut butter on the sides and bottom of each cone. Roll each cone in a shallow dish of birdseed to cover. Tie the pine cones to the tree.

5. Unwrap a suet cake and place in a star-shaped feeder. Set it on top of the tree, pushing it into place among the spoke ends. Secure the feeder with floral wire. Trim sharp wire ends.

6. Secure the tree to the ground with metal lawn staples, or with heavy bricks if displaying on a table or bench.

STAR BRIGHT

These stars and snowflakes are so simple to make. Use them to decorate a tree, wreath or garland, or simply add them to the top of wrapped packages.

WHAT YOU'LL NEED
Small sticks
Embroidery floss, if desired
Hand pruners
Hot glue gun

DIRECTIONS
1. Lay out twigs in snowflake or star designs on a flat surface, trimming as needed with pruners.
2. Using a hot glue gun, attach pieces to one another.
3. If desired, wrap the joints with lengths of embroidery floss, and adhere the ends with a dab of hot glue.

A CHRISTMAS FOR THE BIRDS
Surprise your feathered friends with a holiday treat!

MATERIALS
Tomato cage
Green gardening twine
Fresh greens
Hand pruners
Spray bottle with water, for misting
Fresh cranberries
Strong thread
Unsalted, unbuttered popcorn

Needle
Baker's twine
Pine cones
Peanut butter
Birdseed
Suet cake
Star-shaped suet feeder
Floral wire
Metal lawn staples

DIRECTIONS
1. Turn a tomato cage to rest on its circular top. Bend the spokes together; tie tightly with green gardening twine.

ON POINT

When saws grow worn from cutting down the annual tree, forgo the greenery and hang them as a festive focal point.

MATERIALS
2 old handsaws
Jute ribbon or other decorative ribbon
Decorative embellishments
Tree topper
D-ring with a clip
Heavy-duty, industrial-strength epoxy
Hot glue gun

DIRECTIONS
1. Lay saws side by side, one overlapping the other, in a tree shape, with the teeth facing out and the handles lined up evenly at the bottom.
2. Run a line of epoxy along the right-hand saw's left edge, which will become the vertical center of the tree. Lay the other saw edge on top of the epoxy, pressing until set.
3. Using hot glue, carefully adhere ribbons to the face of the saws in cascading diagonal lines to resemble tree garland. Adhere decorative embellishments and a tree topper.
4. Using epoxy, adhere the clip with the D-ring to the back of the saws near the top. Hang on a wall high enough to be out of reach of small children.

WINE CORK BIRDHOUSE

This might be one of the simplest—yet most impressive—DIY projects you'll ever create because all you really need to know how to do is glue. Just grab a premade birdhouse and let the crafting begin!

By Leslie Concialdi

MATERIALS
Birdhouse
About 50-60 corks
Band saw or serrated knife
Outdoor-grade glue
Dremel tool

DIRECTIONS
1. Cut the corks in half lengthwise with a table band saw or a sharp serrated knife.
2. Glue corks onto birdhouse in any pattern you like, trimming with a serrated knife as needed.
3. Use a Dremel tool or serrated knife to round the corks around the entrance hole.
4. For the roof, glue the cork halves directly on top.

HOMEMADE HELPER
If you want to skip cutting the corks, you can use whole ones. You'll just need more corks and a little more glue per piece.

AWAY IN A MANGER

Use sticks and twigs to build a simple yet lovely stable for your favorite Nativity set.

MATERIALS
¼-in. diameter sticks
Hand pruners
Hot glue gun

DIRECTIONS
1. With hand pruners, cut twelve 5-in. sticks, four 3½-in. sticks and one 4½-in. stick.

2. Hot-glue four 5-in. sticks in a square for the base. Glue one 5-in. stick vertically from each corner. Glue the last four 5-in. sticks in a square and place on top of the vertical sticks to create a cube. Glue the top to the vertical sticks.
3. Hot-glue two 3½-in. sticks diagonally on each side of the top of the cube to create the triangular roof trusses. Glue the 4½-in. stick horizontally at the top to create the ridge pole.

WOODEN PHOTO ORNAMENTS

Bring the outdoors inside with these custom-made accents. Perfect for decorating Christmas trees, they also make wrapped gifts extra special.

MATERIALS

Coaster-size wood slices
Matte-finish photo for each ornament
Thin wood shape for each ornament,
    such as monogram letter, snowflake
    or dog bone as pictured at right
Gloss-finish decoupage glue
Ribbon for hanging loops
Metallic glitter
Small paintbrushes
Spray adhesive
Craft glue
Wood glue
Hand drill
Circle or oval paper punch for
    punching out photos, optional
Clear coat spray sealer, optional

DIRECTIONS

1. If wood slices do not have holes, drill a hole through the top of each, making hole large enough to insert a ribbon for hanging. Wipe off any dust or dirt on wood slices.

2. Using a paper punch or scissors, cut a circular or oval shape from each photo, making sure the shape will fit below the hole on the wood slice.

3. With a paintbrush, apply a thin, even coat of decoupage glue to the back of a wood slice; let dry. Apply an even coat to the front, quickly adhering a photo below the hole, making sure the photo lays flat. Apply 2-3 more thin coats over photo and front of the wood slice, letting glue dry between applications.

4. Repeat with remaining photos and wood slices. Let all pieces dry completely, overnight if needed.

5. Spray a thin coat of adhesive onto the front of each thin wood shape, then cover sprayed side with metallic glitter. Shake off the excess glitter. Let dry completely.

6. Apply a thin line of craft glue around the edge of an ornament photo and sprinkle with glitter. Shake off excess glitter. Use a soft brush or small piece of paper towel to carefully wipe away any remaining glitter.

7. In the same way, add a glitter border to each ornament if desired. Let ornaments dry completely.

8. Using wood glue, adhere desired glittered wood shape onto the back of each ornament. Let dry.

9. If desired, spray each ornament with sealer following the manufacturer's directions for use.

10. Thread a piece of ribbon through each ornament hole. Tie ribbon to create a hanging loop.

HOMEMADE HELPER

These ornaments make great place markers at holiday dinner tables. Or, use them to embellish St. Nick stockings or strands of garland. You can also simply hang them on doorknobs around the house for instant Yuletide flair.

PINE POMANDERS

Old-fashioned decorations get an updated look with craft-room staples.

MATERIALS

Thumbtacks
Ribbon
Styrofoam balls
Small pine cones
Scissors
Hot glue gun

DIRECTIONS

1. Fold a length of ribbon in half and place a thumbtack through the ribbon ends. Apply hot glue to the bottom of the thumbtack; push into Styrofoam ball and apply pressure until set.

2. Find bottom of ball, directly opposite of the top hanging loop. Cut various lengths of ribbon, gather together and push a thumbtack through them all at the middle point. Apply hot glue to the bottom of the thumbtack; push into Styrofoam ball and apply pressure until the glue is set.

3. Adhere pine cones over the entire surface of the ball using hot glue, filling in the voids between with smaller cones.

HOMEMADE HELPER

To create the pretty snowy effect on these pomanders, protect the ribbons by wrapping them up. Lightly spray the entire ball with white spray paint and allow to dry completely. Repeat process with a wall texture spray, using a sweeping motion over the pine cones and letting the spray fall naturally. Allow to dry completely. Finish with a light glitter spray paint and allow to dry completely.

REINDEER GAMES

You know Dasher and Dancer, but "Twiggy" might just become the most famous reindeer of all.

MATERIALS

Sticks of various sizes, from twigs to about 1 in. in diameter
Small red bell
Thumbtacks
Miniature pine cones
Handsaw or hand pruners
Hot glue gun

DIRECTIONS

1. Cut a 1-in.-diameter stick to 3½ in. for the body. Cut a separate 1½-in.-long piece on a diagonal for the head.

2. Cut 4 legs from small sticks about ¼ in. in diameter. Hot-glue to the body.

3. Hot-glue the red bell to the cut edge of the head for a Rudolph nose. Push thumbtacks in for eyes, using hot glue if needed to keep them in place. Hot-glue head to body.

4. Trim down thin twigs to look like antlers. Hot-glue antlers in place on top of the head.

5. Add mini pine cones with hot glue for ears and a tail.

Holiday
HOME DECOR

WHIMSICAL WOOLEN ELF

These fuzzy friends bring elfin magic to any Christmas display. Turn scraps of colorful felt into decorations as warm and comforting as the holiday itself.

MATERIALS (FOR EACH)
12-in. square patterned scrapbook paper
7- to 10-in.-tall papier-mache cone
Decorative fur sheet
Craft felt sheet
Wooden bead
Miniature colored bell
Hot glue gun
Sewing needle and thread, optional

DIRECTIONS:
1. For elf shirt, wrap scrapbook paper around the lower half of the cone. Use hot glue to secure the paper. Trim paper as needed.
2. For beard, cut a raindrop shape from the decorative fur. Trim to desired size proportionate to cone. With the pointed end facing down, use hot glue to secure the beard in place. Allow the beard to overhang the bottom of the cone.
3. For hat, wrap felt sheet around the upper half of the cone, slightly overlapping the beard. Use hot glue to secure hat along the back edge. Trim excess felt as needed. Use hot glue or a needle and thread to attach a bell to the point of the hat.
4. For the nose, use hot glue to adhere a wooden bead to the center of the beard below the hat rim.
5. Repeat steps to create as many felt elves as desired.

HOMEMADE HELPER
These fun fellows are a smart way to use up extra scrapbook paper. Don't have any scrapbook paper on hand? Simply paint the lower half of the cone, dry completely and proceed.

FLOWERS & FRILLS VASES

Dress up old jars with hand-me-down doilies for a lacy new look. To make your vase pop with color, perk up the doily using bright and cheerful fabric dye.

MATERIALS
Mason jars or vases
Doilies or lace
Decorative ribbon, raffia or twine
Spray adhesive

DIRECTIONS (FOR EACH)
1. Thoroughly clean the jar or vase inside and out. Let it dry completely.
2. Measure the doily or lace to cover the exterior of the jar. Trim if needed.
3. Place doily right side down on a work surface. Spray the back side with adhesive. Apply the doily to the jar, smoothing out the wrinkles as much as possible.
4. Decorate as desired with ribbon, raffia or twine.

PILLOW COVER

Here is a simple way to add a fun touch of seasonal flair to your home. Purchase some holiday fabric that complements your decor and make slipcovers for your throw pillows. Best of all, the covers don't take up much storage space after Christmas.

FINISHED SIZE

Pillow cover measures about 17½ in. square.

MATERIALS

1 yd. of 44-in.-wide fabric for pillow cover
18-in. square of muslin or other lightweight fabric for lining front of pillow
All-purpose thread to match fabric
18-in. square of lightweight cotton quilt batting
Quilter's ruler
Rotary cutter and mat
14-in. square pillow form
Standard sewing supplies

DIRECTIONS

1. From fabric for pillow cover, cut one 18-in. square for front of pillow and two 12x18-in. rectangles for pillow back.
2. Place 18-in. square of lining fabric on a flat surface. Center batting on top. Then place 18-in. square of fabric for pillow front right side up on top of batting. Pin as needed to hold. Stitch around outside edges with a scant ¼-in. seam.
3. Press 1 long edge of each rectangle for pillow back ¼ in. to wrong side. Fold and press 1 in. to wrong side and sew close to first fold for hem.
4. Place pillow back rectangles wrong side up on right side of pillow top with outside edges matching and hemmed edges of pillow back pieces overlapping.
5. Sew around outside the edges with a ¼-in. seam.
6. Trim away excess quilt batting in seam close to stitching to reduce bulk. Clip corners.
7. Turn pillow top right side out and press the seams.
8. Topstitch 1½ in. from outside edges of pillow top.
9. Insert pillow form.

A PIECE OF MY HEART

Upcycle old puzzles with this change-of-pace decoration that keeps things merry and bright all winter long.

MATERIALS
Old puzzle
Card stock
Ribbon in coordinating color
Glue gun

DIRECTIONS
1. Draw the outline of a heart on the card stock. Cut along a line ¼ in. outside the outline. Fold the heart in half, and cut along another line ¼ in. inside the outline. Unfold the heart outline.
2. Choose puzzle pieces in preferred color scheme. Hot-glue pieces to the card stock outline, fitting them as close together as possible without overlapping. Glue a second layer of puzzle pieces, covering the seams of the first layer and filling any gaps.
3. Tie a length of ribbon into a bow on the wreath as desired. Alternately, to hang the wreath, loop a length of ribbon through the heart at the top.

GOLD LEAF GLASS VASES

Decorate a table, mantel or shelf with the rich look of gold leaf. These vases make stunning holders for floral arrangements or candles.

MATERIALS

Glass vases of choice
Gold leaf foil sheets
Gold leaf adhesive
Gold leaf sealer
2 medium-width soft bristle or foam brushes
Small soft bristle brush
Masking or painter's tape, optional

DIRECTIONS (FOR EACH)

1. Clean and dry vase thoroughly. Gently tear off pieces of gold foil from sheets, varying the sizes and shapes of pieces for visual interest.
2. If desired, use tape to mark off an edge on outside of vase. Coat the rest of vase exterior with adhesive, using a bristle or foam brush.
3. Let the vase sit for about 20 minutes or until the coating is sticky but not completely dry.
4. Working quickly, apply gold foil pieces using your fingers or another clean foam brush, overlapping pieces at random as desired to add texture. Pat and press pieces until adhered.
5. Remove excess bits with a small dry brush. Carefully remove any tape.
6. Spray the vase with sealer and let dry completely.

HAND-ROLLED BEESWAX CANDLES

These beautiful, long-burning candles brighten up any home, and they make a thoughtful holiday or hostess gift.

MATERIALS

16x8-in. beeswax craft sheets*
2/0 wick (18 in. per pair of candles)

DIRECTIONS

1. Set wax sheets out at room temperature for several hours.
2. Cut desired number of wicks to 9 in. each.
3. Cut wax sheets in half crosswise.
4. For each candle, lay wick along one edge of the wax square, leaving roughly 1 in. of wick extending beyond top edge of the wax. Roll the wax tightly and evenly around the wick, keeping the top and bottom edges of the candle even. Roll completely; press gently along the seam with fingertips to secure.

*Available online. We found them at: *brushymountainbeefarm.com*

• • •

A TREE FOR THE TREE

Dress up your tree, home or office with a small ornament that's tall on sparkle.

MATERIALS

Green, white glitter and
   brown craft felt sheets
Star-shaped bead
Glitter glue
Glitter flake
Embroidery floss in color of choice
Tapestry needle

DIRECTIONS

1. Cut 4 squares each from green felt and 1 from white felt as follows: 2 in., 1¾ in., 1½ in., 1¼ in., 1 in. and ¾ in. Cut five ½-in. squares from remaining green felt. Cut eight ¾-in.-wide circles from brown felt.
2. Lay all of the white squares flat. Apply glitter glue and glitter flake on top. Let dry completely.
3. Stack all brown felt circles. Using a tapestry needle with a long double strand of embroidery floss, stitch through the center of stacked circles to form tree trunk. Do not cut floss.
4. On top of the tree trunk, stack four 2-in. squares of green felt and one 2-in. square of white felt, crisscrossing the corners. Stitch through center of stacked squares to secure in place. Continue the pattern of 4 green felt squares and 1 white felt square, crisscrossing corners. Stack the squares from the largest size to the smallest. Finally, stack the five ½-in. squares of green felt at the top of tree, crisscrossing the corners. Stitch through center of each stacked felt square to secure the layers in place.
5. On top of the tree, stitch star-shaped bead in place. Tie off floss, leaving a strand for a hanger. Loop and knot in place, trimming excess. Finish by twisting squares as needed to replicate the fullness of a Christmas tree.

> ### HOMEMADE HELPER
> To cut the squares more quickly, use a rotary cutter and quilter's ruler on a cutting mat. For circles, a compass fitted with white chalk pencil works well to make outlines. This craft can be adjusted to make larger or smaller trees by scaling all measurements proportionally.

GOT IT COVERED

A painted floor cloth project offers the look of a Christmas quilt—and you don't have to thread a needle!

MATERIALS

Canvas dropcloth
Acrylic paint in desired colors
Fusible bonding web
Clear matte polycrylic finish
Scissors
Iron
Paint brushes
Damp cloth
Foam brush

DIRECTIONS

1. Determine desired size for finished floor cloth. Cut the canvas, adding 2 in. to the length and width for the hem.

2. Iron the canvas to remove wrinkles. Spread the cloth out on a flat surface, with the back of the fabric facing up.

3. Cut strips of fusible bonding web the length of each side.

4. Starting on one side, fold an edge over 1 in. to create a hem. Press with a hot iron to crease. Repeat, creating a hem on each side of the cloth.

5. Place a piece of bonding web inside each fold and lightly press the hem with a damp cloth. Press along the length of each side with a hot iron to fuse the hem.

6. Paint or stencil desired pattern on the front side of the cloth using acrylic paint and brushes. Dry completely.

7. Using a foam brush, apply a coat of polycrylic to seal the floor cloth. Let dry completely.

CHRISTMAS COASTERS

Jazz up any room when you give coffee cups a merry resting spot.

1. Apply **stain** to **wooden coasters** using an old **rag**. Dry completely.

2. Trim **vintage cards** with **scissors** to the coaster size and adhere with **decoupage glue**.

3. Decorate with **holiday-themed stickers** as desired. Apply another decoupage coat to the top.

4. Cut a piece of **adhesive felt** to the coaster size. Peel off the felt backing and apply one piece to the underside of the each coaster.

DECOUPAGED SILHOUETTE PLATES

Arrange these charming home accents on a wall with adhesive plate hangers.

MATERIALS
White plates of various sizes
Scrapbook or other decorative paper
Decoupage glue
Clear matte varnish spray
Cookie cutters or other
  design templates
Paintbrush
Craft knife or scissors
Cutting mat

DIRECTIONS
1. Clean and dry plates thoroughly.
2. Trace cookie-cutter shapes or other design templates separately onto the wrong side of desired scrapbook paper. Cut out paper shapes.
3. With paintbrush, apply a thin coat of decoupage glue over the entire face of a plate, using even strokes.
4. Carefully position a paper cutout where desired on the plate.
5. Using paintbrush, apply a thin coat of decoupage glue over paper cutout to seal. Let dry. Apply another thin coat of decoupage glue over the entire face of the plate, using even strokes.
6. Repeat, adding desired paper designs to the remaining plates. Let the plates dry completely.
7. Spray the plates with a thin coat of clear varnish. Let plates dry completely before displaying.

> **HOMEMADE HELPER**
> Decoupaged plates are not food-safe and are for decorative use only.

SNOWY ETCHED CANDLE VASES

These delightful vases make perfect accents in any room. What a whimsical idea to usher in winter.

MATERIALS
3 clear glass cylinder vases
Desired adhesive-backed
  etching stencils
Painter's tape
Newspaper
Protective gloves
Glass etching cream
Small paintbrush
Clean sponge or paper towel
3 pillar candles
Clear glass bead vase filler

DIRECTIONS
1. Clean vases with soapy water. Let dry completely. Keep areas to be etched clean of all fingerprints and smudges.
2. Adhere a stencil onto a vase where desired, pressing firmly. Rub stencil to make sure there are no air bubbles or wrinkles. Tape down outside edges of the stencil with painter's tape. Rub tape to smooth it down on the glass.
3. In a well-ventilated area, cover the work surface with newspaper. Wearing gloves, follow the cream manufacturer's directions and use a small paintbrush to apply etching cream generously onto open area of the stencil. Brush in at least 2 directions. Leave etching cream on for 15 minutes.
4. Wipe off etching cream with a damp sponge or damp paper towel, removing the cream completely.
5. Carefully remove the stencil and tape from vase. Immediately wash vase with warm water, using a clean sponge or paper towel. Wash vase with soapy water, rinse and dry.
6. Repeat the etching process as needed to add desired etched designs to each vase. Let vases dry completely.
7. Place a candle in each vase; pour glass bead vase filler around candles.

ELFIN MAGIC

These cute magical gnomes put a smile on everyone's face. Best of all, there's no sewing involved!

MATERIALS

Pine cone
1¼-in. wooden craft ball knob
Yarn
½-in. wooden half-ball knob
7-in. felt square
Decorative craft twine
Hot glue gun
Scissors
Needle

DIRECTIONS

1. Hot-glue 1¼-in. wooden ball to the flat bottom of a pine cone.
2. Cut 4-in. pieces of yarn and untwist into separate strands. Hot-glue yarn to ball for a beard. Hot-glue wooden half-ball within the strands for a nose. Trim beard as desired.
3. Roll felt into a cone shape and hot-glue the seam to create a pointed hat. Turn up the bottom of the felt to create a cuff; trim. Hot-glue hat to ball head.
4. Thread twine through the needle and poke through the top of the cap. Knot ends together to hang.

HOMEMADE HELPER

Get creative with these silly little guys. Embellish the hats with festive appliques, tiny bells, small pine cones or even little sprigs of evergreen. Add a tassel or pompom ball near the tip of the hat, or use a glitter paint pen to customize the cuffs with the names of family members. You could also add some plastic googly eyes or try different colors of yarn for the beards.

RANDOM ACTS OF CHRISTMAS HOLIDAY COUNTDOWN

Find an old soda crate, round up some canning jars, then count down to the 25th with one good deed a day.

MATERIALS

Wooden soda crate
24 half-pint Mason jars
Metal barn star for topper
Decorative papers
Chipboard or sticker numbers
Printed sheet of "Acts of Kindness"
    ideas (see list at right)
Trinkets, toys or candy to
    coordinate with paper strips
2 keyhole hangers with
    screws and anchors
Craft glue
Hot glue gun
Power drill
Silver metallic spray paint, optional
Christmas garland, optional

DIRECTIONS

1. Use power drill to install 2 keyhole hangers on back side of crate. Measure and mark for each hole first. For best results, be sure both screws go through the back side of crate and into one of the vertical dividers for the compartments.

2. Use Mason jar lid as a guide to trace and cut out circles from decorative papers. With decorative side facing outward, adhere a paper circle centered on the inside of each lid.

3. Cut out "Acts of Kindness" strips. Fill each jar with a trinket, toy, candy or suggested "Kindness" strip.

4. Screw lids on jars. Center numbers on lids. Adhere with glue. Add garland embellishment if desired. Place the jars in numbered order inside the crate compartments.

5. Add star topper and secure in place with hot glue. (If desired, follow the manufacturer's instructions to paint star with silver metallic spray paint before attaching to crate.)

ACTS OF KINDNESS IDEAS

Celebrate the holidays with tiny acts of kindness sure to brighten anyone's day. Consider these ideas when creating the craft at left, then come up with a few of your own.

- Lift someone's spirit with a merry homemade card.
- Spread some joy and volunteer at a nursing home.
- Wrap or deliver presents for a charity gift drive.
- Make jolly cookies for friends.
- Shovel snow for a neighbor.
- Surprise mail carriers with tiny gifts of candy canes, mini quick breads or homemade fudge.
- Let the person who is in line behind you go ahead of you.
- Donate pet supplies to a shelter.
- Give three or more compliments to others today.
- Hold the door open for a stranger.
- Offer to take someone's shopping cart back into the store.
- Tape money to a vending machine with a note for someone to enjoy a free snack.
- Smile at everyone you pass today.

ECLECTIC MIX

Odds and ends that are too pretty to toss form a one-of-a-kind set of sparkly tabletop tannenbaums. What a unique idea!

MATERIALS

Decorative items such as glass bowls, finials, metal candleholders and goblets
Industrial-strength glue
Mini tree toppers

DIRECTIONS

1. Build a tree shape with decorative items, starting with larger items on the bottom and working up to smaller pieces at the top to create a conical shape.
2. Use drops of industrial glue to adhere the pieces, pressing the pieces together firmly until set.
3. Top each tree with a decorative topper, using glue to adhere.

DRIED FRUIT GARLAND

Spruce up your kitchen with a lovely aromatic garland of cinnamon sticks, bay leaves, pine cones and a variety of dried delights.

FINISHED SIZE
Approximately 30 in. long

MATERIALS
3 navel oranges
2 lemons
2 limes
2 Bartlett pears
3 Red Delicious apples
1 package brown 20-gauge craft wire
1 bag small to medium pine cones
1 spool twine or jute
1 leather upholstery needle
5 cinnamon sticks (about 3½ in. each)
Hot glue gun
1 jar (0.16 oz.) whole bay leaves

DIRECTIONS
1. Preheat oven to 220°. Using a sharp knife, carefully slice the oranges, lemons, limes, 1 pear and 2 apples horizontally, about ¼ in. thick. Slice remaining pear and apple vertically, about ¼ in. thick. Place slices on parchment-covered cookie sheet. Place sheets in oven and bake for 2½ hours. Turn fruit slices and bake an additional 2½ hours or until fruit slices appear dry and edges of apple slices begin to curl. Remove from oven; cool.
2. Cut craft wire into six 5-in. pieces. Wrap a piece of wire around the inside center of each of 6 pine cones, twisting wire to secure.
3. Cut a 55-in. section of twine. Tie a loop at one end. Thread the twine through upholstery needle. Thread twine through the wire of a pine cone. Alternately thread 1-2 fruit slices onto the twine
4. Wrap twine around a cinnamon stick. With a hot glue gun, secure twine on cinnamon stick and cover spot of glue with a bay leaf. Thread 1-2 fruit slices onto twine, alternating different types of fruit and directions of slices.
5. Continue threading with the pine cones, fruit slices and cinnamon sticks; reserving one pine cone.
6. Finish garland with the remaining pine cone and tie a loop in the remaining length of twine.

ICE CANDLES

These lacy-looking candles are easy to make using wax and candle dye—or even old candles! They take a few days to dry, so make them well in advance.

MATERIALS

Clear wax for candle making and candle dye in color of choice or purchased candles in color of choice (see Homemade Helper note)
Double boiler
Matching taper candle for each candle
Commercial candle molds or wax-coated paper cartons
Crushed ice (enough to fill candle molds)
Foil-lined cookie sheet or tray

DIRECTIONS

1. Wash and dry the inside of wax-coated paper cartons. Or prepare commercial candles molds as directed by the manufacturer. (Half-pint milk cartons and commercial molds shown.)
2. Place the molds on foil-lined cookie sheet or tray.
3. In a double boiler over low heat, melt the clear wax and add candle dye in the color of your choice. Or melt purchased candles, removing and discarding the wicks as the wax melts.
4. Pour a few drops of melted wax into bottom of a mold. Immediately place the end of a taper candle into the wax. Let the wax set.
5. Fill the mold with pieces of ice in different sizes and shapes, taking care to keep the taper candle upright.
6. Pour enough melted wax into the mold to cover the ice.
7. Let stand until the wax is hardened and the ice is melted.
8. Pour out the water and carefully tear the carton away or remove candle from commercial mold as directed.
9. Let the candle stand a few days to dry completely before using.
10. If the taper candle is taller than the ice candle, light and allow the taper candle to burn until it is the same height as the ice candle.
11. When using, place the lighted candle on a holder to collect the wax as it melts.

> **HOMEMADE HELPER**
> Estimate how much wax you'll need to fill each carton about half full. Having too much wax is better than not having enough. The ice candles can be scented with fragrance oils. Add the oil to the melted wax in step 3, following package directions. If you plan to use the candles on the dinner table, it is best to leave them unscented.

FELT-WRAPPED CHRISTMAS WREATH

Deck the halls with brightly colored felt! You can choose the colors and the patterns you like best to brighten a door or window.

FINISHED SIZE:
12 in. across

MATERIALS

12-in. wreath form
Various colors of craft felt: green with white polka dots, red with white polka dots, solid red, white glitter
Hot glue gun
Red yarn
Bow
Ribbon

DIRECTIONS

1. Cut 2x6-in. strips of green felt with white polka dots, red felt with white polka dots and solid red felt. Wrap the strips around the wreath form so they overlap. Hot-glue strips to the form. Cut more strips as needed.
2. Cut 2 mitten shapes out of the white glitter felt and 2 smaller hearts and 2 rectangles out of the red felt. Use hot glue to adhere a heart to each mitten; adhere a rectangle to each mitten to form cuff. Use hot glue to adhere a loop of red yarn to the end of each mitten.
3. Use hot glue to adhere the mittens to the wreath and a bow to the upper portion of the wreath.
4. Loop ribbon through the center of the wreath and use it to hang the wreath.

> **HOMEMADE HELPER**
> Keep this no-sew craft in mind when thinking about decor for other holidays. Try pastels and egg shapes for Easter or grab green felt with shamrock cutouts for St. Paddy's Day.

GLASS BOTTLE LUMINARIA

Wondering how you can best upcycle a few old glass bottles, bud vases or Mason jars? Transform them into sparkling luminaria to light up the holiday season. Fill a cluster of them with glittery artificial foliage or even small battery-powered candles.

MATERIALS (FOR ONE)
Glass bottle or jar
Ultra-fine glitter paint
Disposable container for
   mixing paint
Paper plates

DIRECTIONS (FOR ONE)
1. In the disposable container, combine 1 Tbsp. of water with a few tablespoons of ultra-fine glitter paint. Mix well until the consistency is runny.
2. Pour thinned paint into a clean, dry bottle. Swirl paint around bottom of bottle, then rotate bottle on its side, letting paint cover interior of the bottle.
3. When interior of bottle is covered with a thin layer of paint, pour excess paint back into disposable container to reuse if desired.
4. Turn bottle upside down on a paper plate and leave upside down for about 1 hour, allowing additional excess paint to drain. If needed, replace paper plate and continue draining paint for another hour.
5. When paint is tacky and stops running, turn bottle right side up and let dry.

> **HOMEMADE HELPER**
> Regarding the glitter paint, we used DecoArt Glamour Dust Ultra-Fine Glitter Paint for these luminaria.

FOOTSTOOL CUBE WITH POCKETS

Add a splash of fun to your home this year with a useful and stylish footstool. Choose fabrics that fit your holiday decor best.

FINISHED SIZE:

Footstool measures about 16½ in. long by 13½ in. wide by 11½ in. high.

MATERIALS

Plastic storage crate measuring 16½ in. long by 13½ in. wide by 10½ in. high
1-in.-thick high-density foam chair pad
⅞ yd. print fabric for sides
½ yd. print coordinating fabric for top
½ yd. coordinating solid-color fabric for pockets
Standard sewing supplies
Rotary cutter and cutting mat
Sewing machin e

CUTTING

1. Cut the foam chair pad to 16½ x13½ in. to fit the top of the crate.
2. Cut a 17½ x14½-in. rectangle of print fabric for the top of crate.
3. From side print fabric, cut two 17½ x14-in. rectangles for the long side panels and two 14½ x14-in. rectangles for the short side panels. (This includes a ½-in. seam allowance for the tops and sides, 1 in. for the chair pad height and an additional 2 in. for the hem at the bottom.)
4. Cut two 14½ x15-in. rectangles of solid-color fabric for the pockets.

SEWING

1. Fold each solid fabric piece wrong sides together to make 14½ x7½-in. pocket front pieces. Press in place, creasing the fold. Topstitch ½ in. down from the fold. Place each pocket front piece on a short side panel with right sides up and bottom edges matching. Baste or pin in place on bottom and sides.
2. With right sides together and edges matching, pin the 4 side panels together (the 2 with pockets at opposite ends). Use a ½-in. seam allowance and straight stitch to sew as pinned from the bottom up, stopping and backstitching ½ in. from the upper edge, forming a box shape. Press seams open.
3. With right sides together, pin the top fabric panel to the side panels' top raw edges. Using a ½-in. seam allowance and straight stitch, sew the top panel to the sides, pivoting at the corners.
4. For hem around bottom, fold fabric under 2 in. all around with wrong sides together and press in place. Turn edge of fabric under 1 in. Press, pin and topstitch hem all the way around, staying close to inner fold.

ASSEMBLY

1. Flip crate upside down.
2. Place foam on crate.
3. Slide fabric cover over crate and foam.

HOMEMADE HELPER
Feel free to use a larger or smaller crate. Measure the length, width and height of each side. For the four side panel pieces, add a ½-in. seam allowance to the top and side edges, then add 3 in. to the bottom edges to accommodate the 1-in. chair pad and a 2-in. hem allowance. For the top piece, add a ½-in. seam allowance to all four sides.

White vinegar
Clean empty spray bottle
with misting valve
Dropcloth

DIRECTIONS
1. Place the dropcloth over a work surface in a well-ventilated area. Wash and dry the glass vase or candleholder thoroughly.
2. Mix a solution of 1 part vinegar to 1 part water. Fill the squirt bottle with the solution.
3. Shake can of spray paint vigorously for 3-5 minutes.
4. Paint the inside of the glass vase or candleholder as follows: Hold the can close to the glass (no more than 12 in. away) and spray with quick short bursts, working quickly and shaking the can occasionally as you work. Rotate the vase or candleholder as you work until the inside is covered in a thin coat of paint.
5. Let coating dry for 1-2 minutes. Apply a second coat the same as before.
6. Continue adding coats of paint in the same way, letting the paint dry for 1-2 minutes between coats. Apply up to 5 coats if desired.
7. Spray a light mist of the vinegar solution onto the painted area of the glass. Let sit for about 1 minute.
8. Mist a paper towel with the vinegar solution. Gently rub the paper towel over the painted area in small circles, breaking up some of the surface paint. Vary your speed and pressure to mimic the texture of aged mercury glass.
9. Shake can of spray paint vigorously and spray on a final thin coat of paint. Let dry completely.

VELLUM PHOTO LIBRARY

Showcase this three-sided, illuminated display in your home or office.

MATERIALS
Three 5x7-in. photos
Vellum paper
Three 5x7-in. tabletop photo
    frames with straight edges
Adhesive roller or small adhesive dots
Invisible tape
Medical cloth tape
Small battery-operated candle

DIRECTIONS
1. Print 3 separate 5x7-in. photos onto vellum paper.
2. Remove backs from frames. Place a very small amount of adhesive in each corner of the glass on one frame. Gently press a front-facing vellum photo onto the glass, adhering the photo to each corner. Apply invisible tape along the edges in back of frame so that the tape overlaps the photo, securing the photo and glass to frame. Repeat with remaining vellum photos and frames.
3. Lay the 3 frames down side by side with the back sides facing up.
4. Cut a piece of medical cloth tape that is long enough to tape the sides of 2 frames together. Making sure the frames are touching one another, press the cloth tape over the adjacent edges of the first and second frame, taping the 2 frames together.
5. In the same way, tape the second and third frames together.
6. Carefully stand up the connected frames ; bend in the 2 outer frames so their edges touch, forming a three-sided photo luminary.
7. Turn on battery-operated candle and place in the center of luminary.

MERCURY GLASS CANDLEHOLDERS

Here, mirrorlike spray paint produces the look of 19th-century distressed mercury glass.

MATERIALS
Glass vases or candleholders of choice
Krylon Looking Glass
    Mirror-Like spray paint

HOMEMADE HELPER
If you're short on time, try this simple alternative: Spray the glass (inside or outside) with a light mist of water, then quickly apply a coat of spray paint and let dry. The results are similar to, though not as authentic-looking as, the method above that uses vinegar and multiple paint layers.

FELTED BALL DECORATIONS

These woolly spheres are simple to craft from yarn scraps. Roll out a bunch and use them to create heartwarming decorations, such as a cozy wreath or versatile garland.

FINISHED SIZE:
Varies.

MATERIALS (FOR BALLS)
Hollow plastic baseballs, golf balls and/or glass marbles
100% wool yarn and/or roving
Knee-high nylon stockings
Washer (dryer optional)
Liquid dish detergent

(FOR WREATH)
Low-temperature glue gun and glue sticks
Styrofoam wreath base
12-gauge wire
Wire cutters

(FOR GARLAND)
Tapestry needle
Thimble

BALLS
1. Wrap a ball with yarn and/or roving. Wrap even layers over ball until wrapping is about ½ in. thick all around.
2. Stretch stocking carefully and insert a wrapped ball, tying a knot to secure ball tightly in place.
3. Repeat Steps 1 and 2 for desired number of balls. (Each stocking can hold several, with a knot separating each ball.)
4. Wash all of the stockings with a few tablespoons of liquid dish detergent in washing machine using hot water. Repeat if felting is not firm to the touch after the first wash.
5. Air-dry balls or place them in dryer on low heat to dry. Balls may be slightly embedded in stocking. With scissors, carefully work balls free and trim excess fuzz from surface.

WREATH
1. Make desired number of wool balls in a variety of sizes, including marble-size. Hot-glue balls onto wreath base, stacking them randomly to add depth. Let dry.
2. For hanging loop, cut a 4-in. length of wire. Bend it in half and twist the ends together, forming a ½-in. loop. Insert twisted ends into back edge of base and fold the loop over so it is flush against base. Hot-glue loop in place.

GARLAND
1. Make desired number of wool balls. Cut several 5-in. lengths of yarn. With a needle and thimble, thread 1 piece through the edge of 1 ball. Thread same piece through the edge of another ball and tie yarn ends together, forming a loop that connects the balls.
2. Continue joining balls in the same way, forming a garland. On each end, use a yarn piece to make a loop for hanging.

NAPKIN RING PLACE CARDS

Help everyone find their spots with napkin rings that double as table place cards. Guests can take them home for tree ornaments.

Trim down **vintage cards** to fit **precut wood slices** with a hole at the top and adhere with **decoupage glue.** Apply another coat over the top. Add **glitter glue** around the edges. Write guests' names on **blank card stock tags.** Thread **decorative twine** through both the wood slice and the tag and wrap around a **napkin** with the tag and wood slice on top.

MONOGRAMMED BURLAP RUNNER

Transform a piece of plain burlap fabric into a decorative family heirloom using standard sewing and art supplies. You'll want to display this rustic yet refined table runner not only at Christmastime, but all year long.

MATERIALS

Burlap, cut to length of table plus 30 in. (15-in. drop at each end)
Fabric paint
Purchased clear stencils of choice (or make your own—see Note)
Painter's tape
Stiff stencil brush
Small scissors or seam ripper

NOTE: To make your own stencil, use a blank clear stencil (available at craft stores and online) and follow the directions at right. Before stenciling the runner, stencil on a fabric scrap to determine how much paint and pressure to apply. If using the same stencil in reverse for symmetrical designs, wash and dry it completely before reusing it on the runner.

DIRECTIONS

1. To trim the burlap to the desired width for table runner, find a thread at desired width and pull out the thread using small scissors or seam ripper. Cut crosswise threads (see photos at right).
2. Make ½-in. fringe along all edge of the runner by gently removing a few of the edge threads.
3. Lay the runner flat on a large work table. Using tape, secure runner above and below stenciling area.
4. Position the monogram stencil in the center of the runner, about 12 in. from 1 short end. Tape in place.
5. Daub paint onto the burlap using stiff stencil brush, working the paint into the fabric. When the paint is dry, carefully remove stencil.
6. Continue stenciling each short end of runner in the same way as desired, using 1 stencil at a time and securing each with tape. Allow paint to dry before removing each stencil.

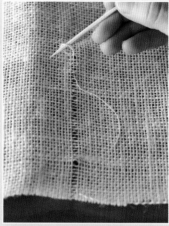

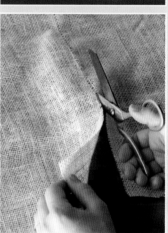

CUTTING MONOGRAMMED BURLAP RUNNER

1. Determine the desired width of runner and choose a thread at the edge of desired width.

2. Using a seam ripper or small scissors, pull the chosen thread to remove.

3. Continue pulling out the thread, creating a line in the burlap at the desired edge of width.

4. Using a small scissors, cut the crosswise threads along the thread line.

HOMEMADE HELPER

To make your own stencil for this project, choose a monogram or other simple shape from a book or other source. Print or photocopy the design to transfer it to a sheet of paper, enlarging or reducing the design to the desired size as needed. Use painter's tape to secure the paper design to a cutting mat. Tape a clear blank stencil on top. Cut out the design from stencil with a craft knife, using a clear ruler or straight-edge guide as needed and applying even pressure for a clean stencil edge.

Whimsical
GIFTS
FOR ALL

PINE CONE FIRE STARTERS

What a festive way to get a fire going! Set a pine cone on your kindling and light a single scale. Gather your own pine cones (let them dry) or buy a bag at a craft store. If you'd like, pretreat them with the additives listed below to produce colored flames. (Be sure to burn only one color at a time.)

MATERIALS
Dry natural pine cones
Clear candle wax
Candle dye colors of choice
Tall tin can and metal tongs
Foil-lined baking sheet
Flame color additives, optional—
   1 cup table salt (yellow flame),
   1 cup borax (yellow-green flame),
   1 cup salt substitute with
    potassium (violet flame),
   1 cup Epsom salts (white flame)

PRETREATMENT FOR COLORED FLAMES (OPTIONAL)
Fill a bucket with 1 gallon hot water. Mix in 1 additive. Soak the pine cones in the solution for 8 hours. Remove; let pine cones dry until fully opened. Dip in wax as directed below.

WAX COATING
Melt the clear candle wax in a double boiler over low heat and mix in desired candle dye. Remove from heat; pour into tall tin can, leaving space near top. With tongs, dip each pine cone into the melted wax until completely covered, then place on foil-lined baking sheet to stand until wax sets.

SEASONAL MAGNET SET

Use store-bought glass pebbles, Mod Podge, and holiday wrapping paper or recycled Christmas cards to create a set of magnets to give as a gift.

MATERIALS
Mod Podge Podgeable Glass Domes
  (6 domes per package)
Mod Podge matte sealer
Foam brush applicator
Assorted holiday paper, gift wrap
  or recycled holiday cards
Construction paper
Rubber stamp
Stamp ink
Clear glitter acrylic paint
Paintbrush
E6000 craft glue
Small button magnets

DIRECTIONS
1. Using assorted papers, gift wrap or recycled holiday cards, find images that you would like to display. Select a glass pebble for each image. Hold glass pebble over its corresponding image; cut around the image so that you have a clean cut and no edges protrude from underneath the pebble. Once all images and designs are cut, sponge the bottom of each pebble with Mod Podge and carefully lay image face down on the pebble. Line up and hold until Mod Podge begins to dry; leave pebble to dry on its own.
2. To create words with glitter, use a rubber word stamp and ink to stamp letters onto construction paper. Let ink dry. Using a small paintbrush and glitter paint, paint a thin coat of glitter over the word so that it can still be read and a thicker coat around the word. Let dry.
3. Once it's completely dry, use the same method above to cut and adhere the construction paper to the underside of a glass pebble.
4. Once the pebbles are dry, apply a dot of E6000 glue to the back of a magnet and carefully affix the magnet to the center back of a pebble. Repeat. Let dry for 24 hours.

NO-SEW CASSEROLE CARRIER

You don't have to be a seamstress to make this unique gift! The sturdy fabric simply folds over the dish and closes with Velcro. Handy straps on each side for carrying make the design even more potluck-perfect.

FINISHED SIZE:
Carrier fits a standard 9x13-in. casserole dish with lid.

MATERIALS:
20x28-in. piece of double-sided fusible ultra-firm stabilizer
Two 20x28-in. pieces of coordinating cotton fabric
$\frac{5}{8}$-in.-wide peel-and-stick Fabric Fuse permanent adhesive
$\frac{5}{8}$-in.-wide ribbon
65-in. length of 1-in.-wide nylon strap
Ruler and fabric pen
Six 2 x4-in. strips of industrial-strength Velcro
Iron and ironing board
Clear tacky glue or Fray Check

• • •

FABRIC BASE

1. Iron both pieces of fabric. Place stabilizer between the pieces with edges matching and right sides facing out.
2. Following stabilizer manufacturer's instructions, iron layered fabrics and stabilizer, fusing all layers into one piece. Trim ¼ in. from all edges, making a 19½x 27½-in. rectangle.
3. Referring to the Assembly Diagram at right, cut a 5x7-in. rectangle from each corner.

ASSEMBLY

1. To cover the raw fabric edges, apply peel-and-stick Fabric Fuse to the back of the ribbon. Fold sticky side of ribbon centered over raw edge. Covering only one straight edge at a time, trim ends flush to fabric. If needed, use glue or Fray Check to prevent cut ribbon ends from fraying.
2. For handle piece, form a loop with the nylon strap. Overlap the ends about 1 in., using peel-and-stick Fabric Fuse to secure in place.
3. Cut 2 Velcro strips in half lengthwise, forming four 1x4-in. strips. Referring to the Assembly Diagram, measure about 3 in. from the bottom of each 7-in.-long flap and place 2 Velcro strips parallel to one another. Place the remaining 2 Velcro strips centered on opposite sides of the nylon loop. Attach each Velcro strip on the loop to a Velcro strip on the fabric, forming handles.
4. Referring to the Assembly Diagram, attach 2x4-in. strips of Velcro on the exterior top corners of the 7-in.-long end flaps. Attach Velcro on the interior top corners of the 5-in.-long side flaps in the same way.
5. Place lidded casserole dish on center of open carrier. Fold over 7-in.-long end flaps, then fold over 5-in.-long side flaps. Secure Velcro to hold casserole dish in place. Wrap handles around the sides to carry.

HOMEMADE HELPER
If desired, stitch down the edges of the Velcro and handle straps to reinforce them. When needed, spot-clean casserole carrier with a damp cloth. Do not submerge in water.

ASSEMBLY DIAGRAM

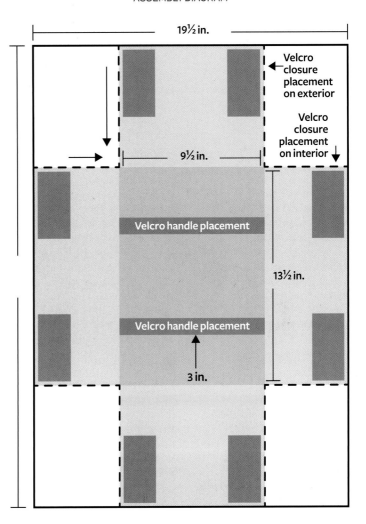

19½ in.

9½ in.

13½ in.

3 in.

Velcro closure placement on exterior

Velcro closure placement on interior

Velcro handle placement

Velcro handle placement

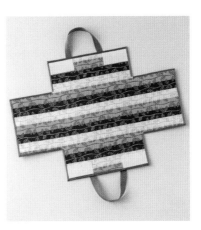

INTERIOR

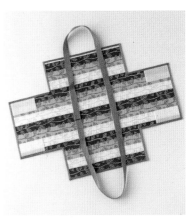

EXTERIOR

BEADED KEYCHAINS

Need a gift for the person who is hard to buy for? Steer your jewelry-making skills in a new direction with these attractive keychains.

FINISHED SIZE
7½ in. long each

MATERIALS FOR GOLD KEYCHAIN (SEE NOTE)
1 gold jump ring
1 gold swivel hook clasp with
    medium key ring
8½ in. of gold oval-link chain
Eight 2-in. gold head pins
1 package assorted seed beads
1 package gold bead caps
Assorted beads in various
    sizes and colors
1 gold medium charm with jump ring
2 gold small charms with jump rings
3 gold lobster claw clasps

MATERIALS FOR SILVER KEYCHAIN (SEE NOTE)
11½ in. of silver oval-link chain
1 silver jump ring
1 silver swivel hook clasp
    with medium key ring
Ten or eleven 2-in. silver head pins
1 package assorted seed beads
1 package silver bead caps
Assorted beads in various
    sizes and colors
1 silver medium charm with jump ring
1 silver lobster claw clasp

NOTE: Both keychains require the use of a side cutter as well as chain-nose, bent-nose and round-nose pliers.

DIRECTIONS FOR GOLD KEYCHAIN
1. Open a jump ring, and attach the key ring of the hook clasp. (To open a jump ring: Position chain-nose and bent-nose pliers on each side of the cut. Bring the tips of one pliers toward you, and push the tips of the other pair away—do not pull the ring side to side. To close the ring, reverse the process.) Measure 4 in. from the top of the chain; slide that link onto the jump ring so one end of the chain hangs longer than the other. Close the jump ring.
2. To make a bead unit: On a head pin, string a seed bead or bead cap. String assorted beads as desired, and make a loop. (To make a loop: Leaving ⅜ in. of pin above the top bead, use side cutters to trim the excess. Using chain-nose pliers, bend the pin to a 90-degree angle. Use round-nose pliers to grasp the end of pin and roll it toward the bead. Reposition pliers and continue rolling to complete the loop.) Repeat to make 8 bead units.
3. To make a charm unit: Open the jump ring of each charm and attach it to the loop of a lobster claw clasp. Close each jump ring.
4. Open the largest charm's lobster claw clasp and attach it to the end of the shortest chain. Attach another charm unit to the middle of the short chain, and attach another toward the top of the longest chain.
5. To attach bead units: Open the loop of the largest bead unit as you would a jump ring, and attach it to end of the longest chain. Continue attaching bead units, varying sizes and spacing them along the chain as desired.

DIRECTIONS FOR SILVER KEYCHAIN

1. Measure 7½ in. from the top of the chain. Cut and open the link to create 2 chains. (To open a chain link or jump ring: Position chain-nose and bent-nose pliers on each side of the cut. Bring the tips of one pliers toward you, and push the tips of the other pair away—do not pull the ring side to side. To close the link or ring, reverse the process.)

2. Open the jump ring, and attach the key ring of the hook clasp and 1 end of the shorter chain. Measure 4 in. from 1 end of the longer chain; slide that link onto the jump ring so 1 end of that chain hangs longer than the other. Close the jump ring.

3. To make a bead unit: On a head pin, string a seed bead or bead cap. String assorted beads as desired, and make a loop. (To make a loop: Leaving ⅜ in. of pin above the top bead, use side cutters to trim the excess. Using chain-nose pliers, bend the pin to a 90-degree angle. Use round-nose pliers to grasp the end of the pin and roll it toward the bead. Reposition the pliers and continue rolling to complete the loop.) Repeat to make 10 or 11 bead units.

4. Open the jump ring of a charm and attach it to the loop of the lobster claw clasp. Attach the lobster claw clasp to the end of the longest chain. Open the loop of the largest bead unit as you would a jump ring (see step 1), and attach it to the end of the shortest chain. Close the loop. Continue attaching bead units, varying sizes and spacing them along the chain as desired.

HOMEMADE HELPER
Consider a shorter "toned down" version of these keychains for the men on your Christmas list.

CUTE LITTLE SOCK CRITTERS

Pick a pretty patterned knee-high sock and create a lovable pet. Make one or all three for a cuddly Christmas surprise.

MATERIALS (FOR ONE TOY):
Pattern diagrams on far right
One knee-high knit sock
Standard sewing supplies
18-mm black plastic nose with screw-on washer
Two 12-mm (for Bunny and Cat) or 15-mm (for Dog) black plastic eyes with screw-on washer
Polyester fiberfill
Tacky glue, optional

NOTE: Due to small parts, these 3 toys are not recommended for very young children. They may pose a choking hazard.

DIRECTIONS
For all sewing, use a ¼-in. seam allowance and coordinating colored thread. Refer to photo and pattern diagrams for cutting and assembly.

DOG
1. Turn sock wrong side out. Mark cutting lines according to pattern diagram. Cut out all pieces.
2. For the legs, fold each piece in half wrong side out, forming 4 rectangles. Sew 1 short side and the open long side, leaving only a short side open on each. Stuff each leg with fiberfill, stitch openings closed and set aside.
3. For body and head, turn right side out. Mark placement of eyes and nose according to pattern diagram. Turn wrong side out. Sew diagonal edge on head, leaving the back end open. Turn right side out. Following manufacturer's instructions, attach eyes and nose. If desired, use a drop of tacky glue on the back of each before screwing on washer to secure in place. Let glue dry. Stuff head and body with fiberfill, stitch back end opening, leaving about an inch open at top to insert tail. (See pattern diagram.)
4. For each ear, with wrong side out sew sides leaving a ½-in. opening, forming two triangles. Turn each right side out. Stuff with fiberfill, stitch opening closed and set aside.
5. For tail, with wrong side out sew sides,

leaving a ½-in. opening, forming a long rectangle. Turn right side out. Stuff with fiberfill, stitch tail opening closed and set aside.
6. Hand stitch legs to bottom of body. Refer to photo above for placement. Insert tail into opening on back end of body and hand stitch to join.

CAT
1. Turn sock wrong side out. Mark cutting lines according to pattern diagram. Cut out all pieces.
2. For body, with wrong side out sew ends and inner edges of legs leaving about an inch opening at the inner edge of one leg. Turn right side out. Stuff body with fiberfill, stitch opening closed and set aside.
3. For head, with right side out mark placement of eyes and nose according to the pattern diagram. Following the manufacturer's instructions, attach eyes and nose. If desired, use a drop of tacky glue on the back of each before screwing

on washer to secure in place. Let glue dry. Turn wrong side out and sew inner edges of ears, leaving about an inch opening their base. Turn right side out. Stuff head with fiberfill, stitch opening closed and set aside.
4. For tail, while wrong side out sew sides, leaving a ½-in. opening forming a long, skinny triangle. Turn right side out. Stuff with fiberfill, stitch opening closed and set aside.
5. Hand stitch head with ears and tail to body. Refer to the photo above for the proper placement.

BUNNY
1. Turn sock wrong side out. Mark cutting lines according to pattern diagram. Cut out all pieces.
2. For arms, fold each piece in half wrong side out, forming 2 squares. Sew 2 of the open sides on each square and turn right side out. Stuff each arm with the fiberfill, stitch the openings closed and set aside.

• • •

3. For legs, fold each piece in half wrong side out, forming 2 long rectangles. Sew 1 short side and the open long side, leaving only a short side open on each. Stuff each leg with fiberfill, stitch openings closed and set aside.

4. For head, with wrong side out sew ends and inner edges of ears. Turn right side out. Mark placement of eyes and nose according to pattern diagram. Following manufacturer's instructions, attach eyes and nose. If desired, use a drop of tacky glue on the back of each before screwing on washer to secure. Let glue dry. Stuff head with the fiberfill and set aside, leaving open at base.

5. For tail, with wrong side out sew sides, leaving a ½-in. opening forming a triangle. Turn right side out. Stuff with fiberfill, stitch opening closed and set aside.

6. For the body, while wrong side out sew the 2 diagonal cut lines, leaving small neck opening unstitched. Turn right side out. Stuff with fiberfill and set aside, leaving neck area open.

7. To join head to body, overlap head base opening about ¼ in. over neck opening on body. Fold bottom sides of open head base in at an angle as shown on diagram. Hand stitch head base to the body.

8. Hand stitch the arms, legs and tail to the body. Refer to photo at far left for proper placement.

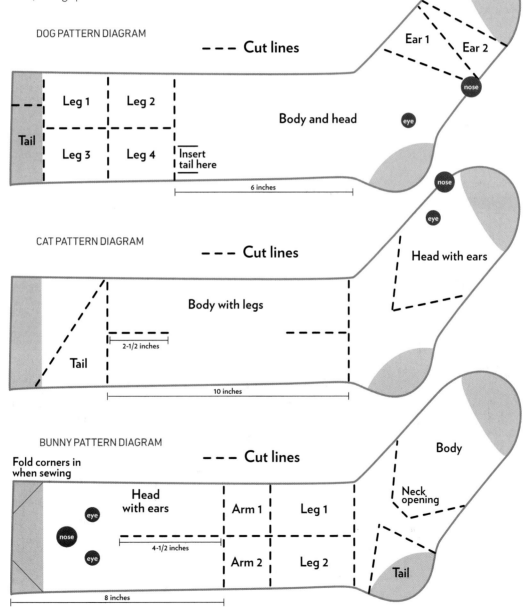

DOG PATTERN DIAGRAM

- - - Cut lines

Leg 1 Leg 2
Leg 3 Leg 4
Tail
Insert tail here
Body and head
6 inches
Ear 1 Ear 2
nose
eye

CAT PATTERN DIAGRAM

- - - Cut lines

Body with legs
2-1/2 inches
Tail
10 inches
Head with ears
nose
eye

BUNNY PATTERN DIAGRAM

Fold corners in when sewing

- - - Cut lines

Head with ears
Arm 1 Leg 1
Arm 2 Leg 2
4-1/2 inches
8 inches
eye
nose
eye
Body
Neck opening
Tail

HANDMADE HEART SACHETS

These sweet potpourri-filled sachets are perfect to give as gifts for Christmas or anytime. What a great way to use extra scraps of fabric.

MATERIALS

Heart patterns (below)
Tracing paper
Fabric scraps
Coordinating all-purpose thread
Trims, optional
Pinking shears
Potpourri
Coordinating button
Ribbon for hanging loop, optional

DIRECTIONS

1. Trace tall heart pattern or wide heart pattern onto tracing paper and cut out. Pin pattern to desired fabric and cut out fabric heart with straight scissors. Unpin pattern and repeat, creating a matching fabric heart.

2. If desired, using all-purpose thread to hand-sew trims to the right side of 1 fabric heart, leaving space to add button at top center point of the heart.

3. Pin together the 2 fabric hearts with right sides out and edges matching. Leaving an opening at the top, machine-sew the fabric hearts together with a ¼-in. seam allowance. Trim edges with pinking shears.

4. Loosely fill heart with potpourri through the top opening.

5. To add a hanging loop, cut a 6-in. length of ribbon, fold in half and insert the ends into the center of the heart opening. Hand-sew the opening closed.

6. Hand-sew button to sachet at the top center point of heart.

HANDMADE HEART SACHET PATTERNS

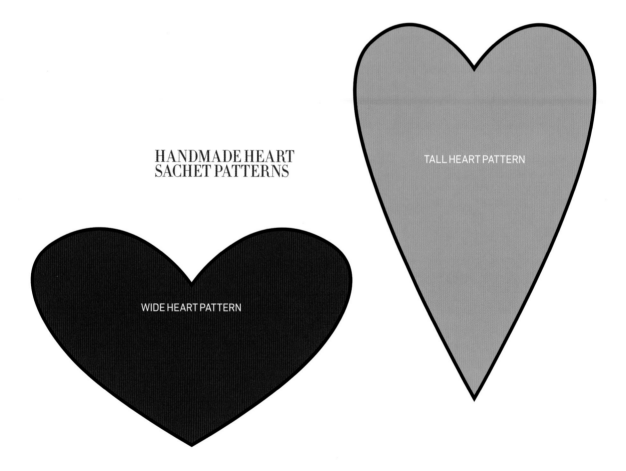

WIDE HEART PATTERN

TALL HEART PATTERN

PINCUSHION & NOTIONS JAR

Want to surprise an avid seamstress? A little fabric and stuffing on the lid of an ordinary Mason jar create a soft spot for pins, while the clear container underneath provides storage for small notions and other tools of the trade.

MATERIALS
Canning jar with screw band and sealer lid
Cardboard
Compass
Fabric scrap
Polyester stuffing
Hot glue
Ribbon, optional

DIRECTIONS
1. Trace the lid of canning jar onto cardboard. Cut out circle and set aside.
2. Using the compass and drawing on the wrong side of the fabric, draw a circle with a diameter that is 2 in. longer than the lid diameter. Cut out fabric circle and set aside.
3. Form a handful of stuffing into a ball. Center it between the cardboard circle and the wrong side of fabric circle. Push fabric through the band until cardboard edge touches the interior band rim and fabric is tightly stretched over stuffing.
4. Fold the excess fabric over cardboard edge and hot-glue to the cardboard.
5. Hot-glue top of sealer lid to cardboard and fabric back. Push firmly in place until glue dries.
6. Hot-glue ribbon to outer edge of band if desired. Let dry.

FRAME EARRING HOLDER

For the gal who has everything, this idea makes a perfect surprise. The fun, easy framed piece accommodates several pairs of earrings.

MATERIALS

6½x8½-in. unfinished wooden photo frame with 4x6-in. opening
Acrylic craft paint
Flat paintbrush
Tacky glue
5x7-in. piece of white needlepoint canvas in size 10 mesh
Tack pins
Paper strips, stickers or other embellishments

DIRECTIONS

1. Use the flat paintbrush to base-coat the frame with acrylic paint. Apply as many coats as needed, letting dry between coats.
2. Cut slits in each corner of canvas piece.
3. Put a line of tacky glue on 1 inner lip of the frame, then align 1 edge of the canvas piece with the glued edge of frame and press into place. Push a tack pin into the canvas piece to secure it while drying.
4. Repeat step 3 for the remaining 3 sides of the canvas piece. Let dry and remove tack pins.
5. Decorate frame as desired with paper strips, stickers or other embellishments.

RECYCLED SWEATER COFFEE SLEEVES

What a cozy idea! Cut pieces from colorful sweaters to make cute wraps for coffee mugs. The simple sleeves open and close with Velcro. If you'd like, use felt instead of a sweater for the personalized label—or skip that detail completely for an easier project.

MATERIALS (FOR ONE):
Patterns at right
4x12-in. or larger piece of a clean bright-colored sweater
2½x4-in. or larger piece of a clean light-colored sweater
3-in.-long strip of ¾-in. sew-on Velcro
HeatnBond light paper-backed iron-on adhesive
Coordinating embroidery floss
Tapestry needle
Standard sewing supplies
1-in.-high or smaller letter stencils, optional

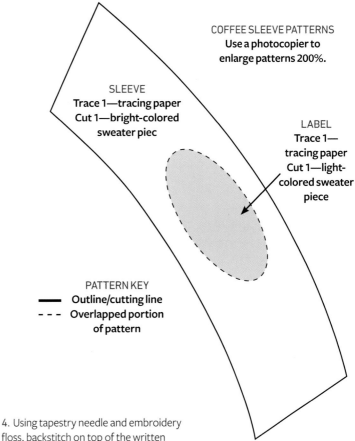

COFFEE SLEEVE PATTERNS
Use a photocopier to enlarge patterns 200%.

SLEEVE
Trace 1—tracing paper
Cut 1—bright-colored sweater piec

LABEL
Trace 1—tracing paper
Cut 1—light-colored sweater piece

PATTERN KEY
—— Outline/cutting line
- - - Overlapped portion of pattern

COFFEE SLEEVE
1. Press sweater pieces flat if needed. Trace sleeve pattern on back of the bright-colored sweater piece and cut out.
2. Either hand stitch or use a sewing machine to sew the Velcro on each short end of the cutout sleeve, positioning the Velcro so that it sticks together when overlapped. Trim ends of Velcro even with edges of sleeve if needed. Set the sleeve aside.

PERSONALIZED LABEL
1. Trace label pattern on back of the light-colored sweater piece and cut out.
2. Trace label pattern on paper-backed iron-on adhesive and cut out. Following adhesive manufacturer's instructions and with edges even, fuse adhesive on back of the cutout sweater label. Leave the paper backing on until the directions state otherwise.
3. Using stencils, if desired, write name or word with pencil on center front of the cutout sweater label, writing lightly so it will not show under the stitching.

4. Using tapestry needle and embroidery floss, backstitch on top of the written name or word, outlining the letters. If desired, use Smyrna cross-stitches as dots or to embellish letters. See Figs. 1-3 at left for stitch illustrations.
5. When finished stitching desired letters, remove paper backing, making sure to remove it from underneath the stitching as well.
6. Lay the open coffee sleeve horizontally in front of you with right side up (sleeve should curve downward to be in the correct position). Lay the label right side up on front of sleeve as shown on pattern above.
7. Following adhesive manufacturer's instructions, use an iron and pressing cloth to fuse the label in place on sleeve.
8. Using tapestry needle and embroidery floss, sew a running stitch all the way around the label about ¼ in. from the edge.
9. To use sleeve, wrap sleeve around coffee mug or cup and secure the Velcro on edges to close.

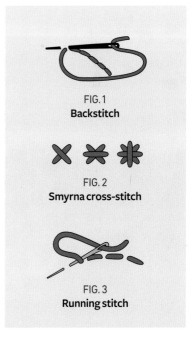

FIG. 1
Backstitch

FIG. 2
Smyrna cross-stitch

FIG. 3
Running stitch

DECOUPAGE COASTERS

These kitchy coasters are sure to add a bit of swanky fun to any holiday happy hour. What a cool gift for today's hosts and hostesses!

MATERIALS (FOR A SET OF 8)

Compass
Two 12-in.-square sheets chipboard in color of choice
Sponge brush
Matte decoupage glue
Several 4½-in.-square scraps of patterned card stock
Polyurethane or waterproof clear sealer

DIRECTIONS

1. Using the compass, create four 4-in. circles on each chipboard sheet. Cut out all 8 circles.
2. Using the sponge brush, coat 1 side of each circle with a thin layer of decoupage glue. Adhere each circle to the back of a card stock scrap. Let glue dry. Trim card stock to the edge of each circle.
3. Coat the top (patterned) side of each coaster with at least 2 layers of matte decoupage glue. Let glue dry to the touch between each layer.
4. Coat the top side of each coaster with a thick layer of clear sealer. Let coasters dry 24 hours before using. To clean, wipe coasters with a damp cloth. Do not submerge in water.

> **HOMEMADE HELPER**
> This is a smart way to use up extra card stock. But be sure the colors and patterns complement one another, as you'll be making an entire set of coasters at once.

A MESSAGE FOR EVERY POT

Ideal for the potluck queen on your list, this customized slow cooker features a chalkboard exterior. Use it to highlight the name of the recipe simmering inside or the ingredients, or make it the center of attention on a buffet with a cute message that guests will adore.

MATERIALS
Slow cooker
Fine-grit sandpaper
Painter's tape
Spray paint primer
Chalkboard spray paint
Chalk or chalkboard markers

DIRECTIONS
1. Remove slow-cooker insert, lid and knobs, making note of the settings that the knobs control, as these may need to be re-marked on the painted cooker if desired.
2. Thoroughly wipe clean the outer surface of slow cooker with a damp cloth. Lightly sand the outer surface using sandpaper.
3. Cover the bottom edge, handles, electrical cord and any other areas that should not be painted. Be careful when taping the curved areas, making sure the tape bonds to the surface so the spray paint cannot seep through.

4. In a protected area, evenly spray outer surface with a thin coat of primer. Allow it to dry thoroughly.
5. Evenly spray the outer surface with 2-3 coats of chalkboard paint, allowing the slow cooker to dry thoroughly between coats.
6. When last coat of paint is dry, carefully remove tape. Reattach knobs; insert liner and lid. Write a message on the outside of the slow cooker as desired using chalk or chalkboard markers.

• • •

CATNIP MOUSE TOY

Furry felines (and their owners) will think this toy is the cat's meow. Choose colorful fabrics for extra fun. No sewing machine is needed—simply stitching by hand will do.

MATERIALS (FOR ONE)
4¼-in. circle of fabric
Coordinating felt for ears
Coordinating all-purpose thread
5-in. length of jute twine
Black 6-strand embroidery floss
Dried catnip
Hand-sewing needle
Embroidery needle

DIRECTIONS (FOR ONE)
1. Fold the fabric circle in half with the right sides together.
2. Sew along the raw edge of fabric, using a ¼-in. seam allowance and leaving a 1½-in. opening at one end.
3. Turn the fabric body right side out. Fill with catnip.
4. Insert ½ in. of twine piece into the opening, leaving a 4½-in. tail. Fold in fabric edges and sew opening closed. Sew through twine 3-4 times to secure.
5. Separate strands of floss and cut six 4-in. strands. Thread embroidery needle and run floss through the tip of mouse's head for whiskers. Knot floss on either side of head. Separate strands and trim to desired length.
6. Thread an embroidery needle with 2 strands of floss. On each side of head, backstitch several times about ½ in. above the whiskers to form the eyes.
7. To make ears, cut 2 felt half-ovals measuring ½ in. across the straight edge and 1 in. at highest point of curve. Pinch each ear at the center of straight edge and sew to the top of body about 1 in. behind the eyes.

STAMPED METAL PET TAG

Don't forget Fido this holiday season. A handmade dog tag is a wonderful way to include furry friends in on the fun.

MATERIALS
Blank metal circular tag, about 1½ in. across (sterling silver, aluminum, stainless steel or copper)
Metal letter stamps
Flat-headed hammer for stamping metal
Metal or steel bench block
Extra fine-tip black marker
Fine sandpaper
Metal hole punch
Beads and metal charms of choice
Metal head pins (for beads and charms)
Masking tape
Wire cutters
Long-nose pliers
Small key ring

DIRECTIONS
1. Place the metal tag on bench block and secure in place with masking tape.
2. Lightly mark where you will stamp each letter of the name on the metal tag, starting with the center letter and working to the left and right so that the name will be centered.
3. Place metal stamp so that the head of the stamp is completely flush with the metal tag. Strike the stamp once with the hammer. Repeat if needed, making sure not to move the stamp from its original position. Continue stamping all letters.
4. Using the black marker, color in the impressions of all stamped letters on the metal tag.
5. Using fine sandpaper, gently sand the tag to give it a polished look.
6. Punch a hole in the tag and attach tag to key ring.
7. Place desired beads or charms on a head pin. Use wire cutters to cut off any excess length of head pin. With pliers, curve remaining end of head pin and attach securely to the key ring.
8. If desired, add more beads or charms to head pins and attach to the key ring the same as before. Attach key ring to metal ring on pet collar.

BARN ANIMAL PUPPET SET

This wooden one-of-a-kind play set is perfect for little fingers. Use your imagination and a little creativity to add even more animals or paint the puppets to resemble family members.

MATERIALS
Patterns at far right
Acrylic craft paint—very dark brown, medium brown, very light brown, porcelain, white, green, yellow and pink
Flat paintbrush
Craft foam scraps—gray, black, very dark brown, medium brown, orange, dark pink and blue
Ten 5-mm wiggle eyes
Quick-drying tacky glue or super glue
Toothpicks
Premade unfinished wooden toy barn
Five 1¼-in.-high wooden candle cups
Five 1-in. wooden doll heads
1½-in. wooden block
2-in. wooden block

Two 1½-in.-wide wooden circles
Two 2-in.-wide wooden circles
Two ⅜-in. wooden buttons
Fine-point black permanent marker
Compass

FINGER PUPPETS
1. For each finger puppet, glue the flat edge of a doll head onto the bottom of a candle cup. Let dry.
2. Base-coat each finger puppet with acrylic paint, using white paint for the sheep, yellow paint for the chick, very light brown paint for the bull, pink paint for the pig and desired color of paint for the farmer. Apply coats as needed for full coverage, letting dry between coats.
3. Trace black outlines of patterns onto foam as directed on patterns. Cut out pieces. Glue gray nose and black ears onto the sheep's head. Glue beak and feathers onto chick's head. Glue horns, medium brown nose and medium brown ears onto bull's head. Glue dark pink nose and ears onto pig's head. Glue mustache onto farmer's head.

4. Cut a 3½x¾-in. strip from blue foam, then cut the ends at an angle. Glue foam around the farmer's body for the vest, overlapping the ends to form a slight "V" shape at the neck.
5. Cut a 3x½-in. strip of very dark brown foam. Roll into a circle, overlap ends about ¼ in. and glue in place. On very dark brown foam, use compass to draw a 1½-in. circle, then draw a ¾-in. circle in the center, making a doughnut shape. Cut out shape for hat brim. Glue rolled circle centered on top of brim. Glue hat on farmer's head.
6. Glue a set of wiggle eyes centered above the nose on each animal and above the mustache on the farmer.
7. Referring to the patterns, use marker to draw mouths and noses on puppets.

BARN AND TRACTOR

1. Base-coat the wooden barn with medium brown paint. Apply as many coats as needed for full coverage, letting dry between coats.

2. Base-coat the remaining wooden pieces, using green paint for the blocks, very dark brown paint for the circles and yellow paint for the buttons. Apply as many coats as needed for full coverage, letting dry between coats.

3. For the tractor body, center and glue the small block on one side of the large block, making one side of small block flush with one side of large block. (The flush sides are the bottom of tractor.) Glue buttons centered, side by side, on front of small block for lights. Glue a small circle on each side of the small block for front wheels. Glue a large circle on each side of the large block for back wheels. Let dry.

FINGER-PUPPET PATTERNS

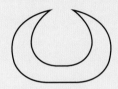

BULL, SHEEP AND PIG EARS
Cut 2 each—medium brown, black and dark pink foam

BULL HORNS
Cut 1—very dark brown foam

BULL NOSE
Cut 1—medium brown foam

SHEEP NOSE
Cut 1—gray foam

PIG NOSE
Cut 1—dark pink foam

CHICK FEATHERS AND BEAK
Cut 1 each—orange foam

FARMER'S MUSTACHE
Cut 1—very dark brown foam

KNIT CELLPHONE COZY

Who wouldn't love to tote their cellphone in this cute little holder? Because the knit cozy is felted, you can cut a simple working buttonhole without having to stitch it. For faster access to a ringing phone, use a Velcro strip or snap instead, making the button on the flap purely decorative.

MATERIALS
100% wool yarn
Size 9 knitting needles
2 size 9 double-pointed needles
Sewing needle and thread
**   to match yarn**
Velcro strip or snap closure, optional
Coordinating button

PRE-FELTED SIZE
The base is 5¼ in. wide by 8 in. long.
**   The flap is 4 in. wide by 3½ in. long.**

FINISHED SIZE
The base is 4 in. wide by 5¼ in. long.
**   The flap is 3 in. wide by 2½ in. long.**
(Overall shrinkage rate is about 30%. We recommend making a felted swatch to check the gauge and shrinkage rate before making the cozy. Different wool yarns may vary in shrinkage rate.)

SPECIAL STITCHES
Stockinette stitch:
**   Row 1 (right side): Knit**
**   Row 2: Purl**
**   Repeat Rows 1 and 2**

BODY (STARTING AT BOTTOM)
Cast on 30 stitches.
Row 1: Knit one; slip one (as if to purl) across the row, ending with a slipped stitch. Turn. Continue as in Row 1 for another 55-60 rows (or until about 8 in. long), making an open tube.

FLAP
Put the slipped stitches onto 1 double-pointed needle and the knit stitches onto the other double-pointed needle, allowing the tube to open. With No. 9 needle, bind off the first 15 stitches, then work the other 15 stitches in stockinette stitch for 16 rows (or until about 3½ in. long), making the flap. Bind off; weave in ends.

FELTING
1. Set a top-loading washing machine to the smallest capacity on a hot-water wash cycle. Place cozy in a pillowcase or mesh bag for protection, then place protected cozy, liquid detergent and a few old towels or pairs of jeans (to create some agitation) in washing machine.
2. Wash in hot water for 10-15 minutes to allow shrinkage.
3. Stop washer and remove the cozy. If needed, gently rub cozy horizontally and vertically to continue felting by hand until desired size is achieved.
4. Rinse cozy in lukewarm water to wash out remaining soap. Shape cozy by hand as desired and lay flat to dry. (Do not apply heat to dry.)

FINISHING
1. If a buttonhole closure is desired, cut a buttonhole in the center of the flap (stitching is not necessary; felted wool will not ravel). Sew the button on the corresponding area of the cozy body.
2. If a Velcro or snap closure is desired, sew the Velcro or snap centered on the underside of flap and the corresponding area of cozy body. Sew button on the outside of flap for decoration.

> **HOMEMADE HELPER**
> Did you accidentally knit or purl instead of slipping a stitch? There will be a little closed spot in the tube where you did this. Just go ahead and felt it anyway. Once it is felted, you can carefully cut the closed stitch. Felted wool will not ravel.

SCRAPPY RIBBON FLOWERS

Up your gift-wrapping game with these eye-fetching flowers. Turn scraps of ribbon or fabric into pieces of art you can use in place of bows, or you can attach a hair clip for a wearable accent.

MATERIALS (FOR ONE):
1-in.-wide ribbon or fabric strip
Extra-large circle glue dot (1 to 2 in.)
Additional smaller glue dots
Scrap of card stock

DIRECTIONS (FOR ONE)
1. Adhere an extra-large circle glue dot onto card stock; carefully cut out around the glue dot.
2. Fold ribbon or fabric strip in half to measure about ½ in. wide. Adhere 1 end to outer edge of extra-large glue dot.
3. Keeping the folded edge up, adhere the open edge to the glue dot, spiraling inward toward the center and using small glue dots to secure the edge as needed.
4. At the center, trim the remaining end to about 1 in. and make a loop. Use small glue dots to secure loop in the center.

SWEET PAINTED MUGS

Cheers! Easy-to-use paint pens create fun and colorful designs on white coffee mugs for these cute gifts

MATERIALS

2 white ceramic coffee mugs (see Note)
Cookie cutters to use as patterns—gingerbread man, large circle and small circle
Scrap paper
Temporary spray adhesive
Oil-based paint-pens—gold, pink, orange, yellow, green, blue and white
Goo Gone cleaner to remove adhesive
Cotton applicator or small sponge applicator

DIRECTIONS

1. Wash coffee mugs and let dry completely.
2. For patterns, trace gingerbread cookie cutter on scrap paper and cut out. Trace large circle cookie cutter onto paper, then trace small circle cookie cutter in the center to create a doughnut shape. Cut out doughnut.
3. Lightly spray temporary adhesive on back of the gingerbread pattern and gently adhere the pattern to a coffee mug where desired, smoothing down the edges.
4. Randomly paint small dots around the gingerbread pattern using paint pens in a variety of colors, placing dots closer together along the edge of the pattern. Continue adding dots until they form an obvious gingerbread man outline. Let dry. Carefully remove the pattern.
5. Repeat with the doughnut pattern and remaining mug the same as before. Trace outline of doughnut using gold paint pen. Let dry. Remove pattern.
6. Use cotton or sponge applicator and Goo Gone to remove any remaining adhesive on both mugs.
7. Use white paint pen to paint the glaze on the doughnut, applying 3-4 coats and letting the paint dry after every application.
8. When painted glaze is dry, randomly add sprinkles on doughnut using paint pens in a variety of colors. Let dry.
NOTE: Painted coffee mugs are not dishwasher- or microwave-safe.

CHALKBOARD PLAY MAT

Ideal for keeping little ones occupied in the car or waiting room, these simple play mats roll up for moms on the go.

MATERIALS

16-in.-square piece of duck cloth in desired color
12-in.-square piece of chalk fabric
36-in. length of ⅜-in.-wide ribbon
Standard sewing supplies
Iron with pressing cloth
Chalk

DIRECTIONS

1. On all sides of the duck cloth square, fold a ¼-in. hem with the wrong sides together. Use iron with pressing cloth to press in place, then fold a 1½-in. hem with wrong sides together and press the hem in place.
2. Unfold both the 1½-in. and ¼-in. hems. Cut out the small square crease at each corner. Fold in the cut corner edges diagonally and press in place to form mitered corners.
3. Refold ¼-in. and 1½-in. hems. Press in place. (The diagonal corner edges should meet, forming a line. Adjust mitered corners if needed for alignment.)
4. Insert the chalk fabric right side up and centered under the folded edges of the duck cloth. Smooth the chalk fabric so it lies flat on the duck cloth with the folded edges overlapping.
5. Using a straight stitch, sew ¼ in. from inner edge of duck cloth around the perimeter of chalk fabric. Using a zigzag stitch, sew along each mitered corner where duck cloth forms a diagonal line.
6. Fold ribbon in half. Place folded end of ribbon so it overlaps straight stitch about ½ in. on center of one side of the mat. Sew ribbon in place on top of existing straight stitch to form a loop for the chalk. Use remaining length of ribbon to tie mat in a roll.
7. Before using, prep chalk fabric by rubbing with the side of a piece of chalk and wiping with a dry cloth.

SWEATER BACKPACK

What a great way to upcycle wool sweaters. This adorable backpack is a gift that keeps on giving. It stands at roughly 13½ inches, making it perfect for kids.

MATERIALS

Two coordinating adult-size recycled all-wool sweaters
Matching all-purpose thread
Magnetic purse closure
Four 1-¼-inch metal D rings
½-inch x 40-inch coordinating cloth or leather strip for tie
1-¼-inch coordinating button for flap
Standard sewing supplies

FELTING

1. To felt the sweaters, machine-wash them in hot water using laundry detergent, running them through a complete cycle that includes a cold rinse cycle. Without using detergent, repeat this process until the sweaters are felted as desired.
2. Smooth out wrinkles and place felted sweaters on a flat surface to dry. Check sweaters while drying and smooth them out as needed.

CUTTING

1. Cut two 14x15-in. pieces from body of 1 sweater for the front and back of backpack. From sleeves, cut two 3x10-in. strips and two 3x28-in. strips for the straps. (Strips may need to be joined to make the two 28-in. long straps.) Cut a 5½x10½-in. piece for the outside of the flap.
2. From the coordinating sweater, cut a 5½x10½-in. piece for the lining of the flap. Also cut a 4x11-in. piece for the bottom.

STRAPS

1. Fold long edges of a 3-in.-wide strip for strap with wrong sides together and edges meeting in the center to make a 1½-in.-wide strap. Pin as needed to hold in place. Sew down the center of the strap with a wide zigzag stitch, catching the edges of each side in the stitching. Repeat with the remaining strap pieces to make two 10-in.-long straps and two 28-in.-long straps.
2. Round 1 end of each strap and overcast edges.
3. Thread 2 D rings on the rounded edge of each of the 10-in.-long straps. With wrong sides facing, fold rounded edge back 3 in. Sew ends in place on each strap to secure D rings.

FLAP

1. Following manufacturer's instructions, attach 1 half of magnetic purse closure to right side of the coordinating (lining) flap piece centered 2 in. from 1 narrow end.
2. Pin the outside and inside flap pieces together with right sides facing and edges matching. Sew pieces together with a narrow seam, rounding the corners on the end with magnetic closure. Trim excess and turn flap right side out.
3. Topstitch ½ in. from the edge of flap if desired.
4. Hand-sew button to right side of flap over magnetic closure.

ASSEMBLY

1. Pin the two 14x15-in. pieces for the front and back of the backpack together with the right sides facing and edges matching. Sew the long edges together with a ¼-in. seam for sides of backpack. Overcast the raw edges.
2. Fold 1 in. along top edge to wrong side. Zigzag close to raw edge for the hem. (If the fabric is too stiff, then the hem can be omitted.)
3. Center the straight edge of the flap about 2 in. from the top back top edge of right side of backpack. Top stitch close to raw edge of flap and then stitch ¾ in. from the first row of stitching to form a channel.
4. Sew raw edge of straps with D rings centered along the raw edge of flap on the right side of back of the backpack.
5. Starting about ½ in. from sides of flap on back, cut 4 evenly spaced ½-in. slits in the front and back of the backpack for leather strip.
6. With wrong side of 28-in.-long straps facing right side of the back, pin straps 1-½ in. from side seams of back. Sew straps in place with a narrow seam.
7. Pin bottom piece to bottom edge of backpack with right sides facing, and side seams centered on the opposite short sides of bottom piece. Ends of straps will be sandwiched between backpack and bottom piece. Sew bottom piece to backpack with a ½-in. seam. Leave needle down at each corner, turn and realign the raw edges as you continue to sew. Sew around a second time to reinforce the seam and then overcast the raw edges. Turn backpack right side out.
8. Thread end of a long strap through both the D rings on corresponding short strap. Then thread the end through just 1 of the D rings to secure. Repeat with the remaining straps and adjust to the desired length.
9. Starting at the front, thread the leather or cloth strip in and out of the slits and through the channel on the back of the backpack. Tie ends in front.

> **HOMEMADE HELPER**
> The most important thing for a recycled sweater project is to look for interesting sweaters, whether it is a thrift-store find or an unused one from your closet. Consider using a printed sweater and coordinating solid-color sweater for a great backpack.

Impressive
JEWELRY
IDEAS

CUFF BRACELET

This cuff looks like leather but is made of sturdy grunge paper. Vary colors and stamps to suit those on your list.

MATERIALS

Grunge paper
Two different Tim Holtz Distress Inks
Ink-blending tool
Stamps
Embossing powder
Embossing heat tool
Decorative-edge scissors or paper cutter, optional
Hook-and-eye clasp
Standard sewing supplies
Paper towels

DIRECTIONS

1. Cut an 8x2½-in. piece of grunge paper. If desired, use decorative scissors or paper cutter to trim one side of paper strip in a wavy pattern.
2. Lay grunge paper on paper towels. Add ink horizontally along the length of each edge as follows: Dab ink-blending tool onto Distress Ink pad, then rub tool onto grunge paper in a circular motion, transferring ink. Use inks of different colors along each edge. Let dry.
3. Decorate grunge paper as desired with inked stamps. While the ink is still wet, sprinkle embossing powder on the designs, shaking off excess powder. Following manufacturer's instructions, use heat tool to set embossing powder. If paper edges curl during heating, gently shape flat again while still warm.
4. Use standard scissors to round off end corners. Sew hook-and-eye clasp centered on ends of cuff.

CHUNKY SILVER BRACELET

Cinching a silver chain creates the base of this eye-catching accent. Beads in various hues of blue add a frosty look.

MATERIALS

12-in. length of beading wire (or desired length of bracelet plus 4 in.)
Beading needle
78-in. length of small open-loop silver chain
24 silver head pins
Twenty-four 6-mm beads
2 silver clam clasps
Silver toggle clasp with jump rings
Round-nose pliers
Chain-nose pliers
Wire cutters
G-S Hypo cement or jewelry glue

DIRECTIONS

1. Thread needle with beading wire and tie the wire ends in a knot close to the end. Use wire cutters to trim excess wire close to knot.
2. Thread the unknotted end of wire through the hole in one end of a clam shell until the knot rests inside shell. Add a drop of glue to secure. When dry, use the chain-nose pliers to close and secure clam clasp.
3. Thread the needle through every other loop on the silver chain, drawing up the loops close to each other.
4. Thread remaining clam clasp onto wire. Tie a knot as close as possible to chain, making bracelet about 7 in. long or desired length. Add a drop of glue to secure. When dry, use chain-nose pliers to close and secure clam clasp.
5. Insert a head pin in a bead. Attach the bead to chain where desired, using round-nose pliers to make a loop close to the top of the bead. Trim excess. Repeat to add remaining beads.
6. Attach the toggle clasps to the clam clasps at the opposite ends of bracelet.

> **HOMEMADE HELPER**
> For this bracelet, we used a combination of clear, frosted, light blue and ice blue beads.

GREEN DANGLE EARRINGS

Christmastime will shine bright with these beaded earrings. They are easy to customize for friends using beads in the recipient's favorite colors.

MATERIALS
2 French hook earrings
14 green smooth briolette beads
Fourteen 2-in. lengths of
  gold jewelry wire
2½-in.-long medium gold chain
Wire cutters
Round-nose pliers
2 pairs of flat-nose pliers

> **HOMEMADE HELPER**
> We used a gold chain with alternating large and small links.

WIRED BEADS

1. Slide a bead about a third of the way onto a 2-in. piece of gold wire. Bend both ends of the wire over the bead, forming a triangle about ⅛ in. from top of bead.
2. Using flat-nose pliers, grab the longer end of wire and bend it straight up over the bead. Next, grip the pliers over the wire triangle shape, clasping both sides. With the second pair of flat-nose pliers, grip the shorter end of wire and wrap it around the longer end once. Cut off any excess.
3. Using flat-nose pliers, grab the longer end of wire just above the wrapped wire and bend the longer end, making a right angle. Put the round-nose pliers about ⅛ in. away from the right angle with your wrist upside down. Pull the end of the wire over the pliers until it is parallel with the bead, then roll your wrist forward, forming a rounded hook shape (see figure at above right). Do not close it off into a loop or cut the end.

4. Repeat steps 1-3 to make 7 wired beads for each earring.

ASSEMBLY

1. To form a chain piece for each earring, use the wire cutters to cut the 2½-in.-long chain in half. If you have 2 different sized links on the chain, leave the first small link empty.
2. To attach a wired bead to the earring chain, string the open loop onto a link. Then clamp onto the loop with flat-nose pliers. With the second pair of flat-nose pliers, grip the end of the loose wire and wrap it around the space between the loop and the bead about 2-3 times, cutting off any excess wire. (This attaches the bead to the chain link.)
3. Following the instructions in step 2 and starting with the top large link on each chain, attach a total of 7 wired beads on each earring chain, spacing the beads evenly along the links. (For bead spacing, use 2 beads on the first link, 1 on the second link, 2 on the third link, 1 on the fourth link and 1 on the fifth link.)
4. To attach the French hooks, use flat-nose pliers to pull the loops on each hook slightly open. For each earring chain, slip the first chain link onto a French hook loop. Using flat-nose pliers, close the French hook loop.

MEMORY WIRE BRACELETS

Stacked together or worn individually, these stylish accessories are fun-to-wear any season. Plus, the versatile bracelets are simple enough for beginners to create—without much expense or the toolkit of a highly experienced jeweler.

MATERIALS (FOR ONE)

Plated memory wire (large bracelet size)
Desired beads or crystals
Round-nose pliers
Wire cutters
Beading board, optional

DIRECTIONS (FOR ONE)

1. Using wire cutters, cut a piece of memory wire about 4 loops long for a 4-strand bracelet (or cut a longer or shorter piece as desired).
2. Grasp one end of memory wire with round-nose pliers and curl wire tightly around one side of pliers. Wrap a few times to form a sturdy closed circle.
3. If desired, use a beading board to create the desired pattern for beads. String the desired number of beads onto memory wire, starting at the end without the circle.
4. When all beads are in place, trim the memory wire about ½ in. from the base. Grasp the end of wire with round-nose pliers and wrap wire around pliers a few times as before, forming a sturdy closed circle that is snug against the last bead.

CROCHETED WIRE BRACELET

This lovely bracelet starts with an easy idea. Simply crochet basic stitches with thin wire, adding beads as you go.

MATERIALS

40 or more assorted small beads
2 medium metal beads
Clasp with jump rings
9 yds. of 26-gauge wire
Wire cutters
Flat-nose pliers
Size J/10 (6-mm) crochet hook
Clear tape

DIRECTIONS

1. Use wire cutters to cut wire into six 54-in. pieces.
2. Tie a slipknot on one end of each wire piece, leaving a 3- to 4-in. tail.
3. Use crochet hook to make each wire piece into a chain, making about 3 chains per inch and sliding a small bead onto every fourth chain. Make each of the beaded chains about 6½ in. long with a 3- to 4-in. tail on each end.
4. Working just above the first chain on each wire, twist the tails of the wires together tightly a few times. Use tape to hold the twisted ends in place.
5. Leaving the taped ends together, slightly separate the crocheted wires into 3 groups of 2 wires each. Working with each group as 1 strand, braid the 3 groups together.
6. When finished braiding, twist the loose tails together very tightly. Remove the tape from opposite end and twist those tails in the same way.
7. Form each twisted end into a flattened loop about ½ in. long. Tightly twist the base of each loop to secure it in place. Push each loop through a medium metal bead. Trim the excess wire at the base of the loop.
8. Use pliers to open the jump ring on individual parts of the clasp. Place a jump ring on each loop. Use pliers to close the rings and to secure the toggle clasp parts in place.

STAMPED PENDANT

Turn a pendant blank into an extra-special gift with a simple metal-stamping technique.

MATERIALS

Metal pendant blank
Scrap sheet metal or blanks (for practice)
⅛-in. alphabet metal stamp set
⅛-in. heart or other metal stamp symbol, optional
Hammer
Jeweler's anvil or metal bench block
Metal hole punch
Long-nose pliers
Round-nose pliers
Wire cutters
Jeweler's polishing pad
Permanent fine-point black marker
6-mm or larger metal jump rings
Head pins
Small beads or crystals
Necklace chain

PREPARATION

1. Clean the surface of the pendant blank and any practice sheet metal or blanks.
2. For a centered word design, count the number of letters in the word and divide in half, identifying the center letter or letters. (If the design contains a symbol, count it as a letter.) On the front of the pendant blank, use permanent black marker to mark small dots for each letter or symbol position, marking from the center letter outward and leaving about ⅛ in. of space between each mark. (If random placement of letters or symbols is desired, no marking is necessary.)

STAMPING

1. Before stamping desired pendant blank, practice using the alphabet metal stamps a few times on scrap sheet metal or blanks.
2. Lay pendant blank flat on jeweler's anvil or metal bench block.
3. Using the marked dots for placement and beginning with the center letter, align the alphabet stamp vertically on top of mark. Holding the stamp in place against surface, use hammer to firmly strike top of stamp. (If possible, do not strike more than once to avoid a double image. If one strike does not make a complete impression, be sure the stamp is aligned before striking a second time.)
4. Repeat step 3 for each letter, working outward from the center mark.

COLORING

1. Use permanent black marker to color in the recessed areas of each stamped letter. (It's fine to get marker slightly outside recessed areas.)
2. Use jeweler's polishing pad to gently rub the surface of the pendant, removing excess marks. (The color should remain in recessed areas. If needed, use marker to lightly fill in areas that are not dark enough.) Wipe metal clean.

DANGLING CHARMS

1. Place bead or crystal onto a head pin.
2. With bead or crystal firmly in place at bottom of head pin, bend head pin wire at a 90° angle against the top of the bead or crystal. Use wire cutters to clip wire about ¼ in. from bend.
3. Placing round-nose pliers at wire end, roll the wire over, forming a closed loop. If needed, reposition pliers mid-roll to complete the loop.
4. Repeat steps 1-3 to create the desired number of dangling charms.

FINISHING

1. If needed, use metal hole punch to make a hole in stamped pendant.
2. Use long-nose pliers to open a jump ring by carefully twisting sideways where ring ends meet (do not pull apart). Slip open jump ring through hole on stamped pendant. Place dangling charms onto same jump ring (if large enough) or onto separate jump rings. Use long-nose pliers to twist jump rings closed.
3. Slip the pendant and charms onto a necklace chain.

> **HOMEMADE HELPER**
> Over time, the black marker may wear off recessed areas. Repeat the coloring process if needed.

PHOTO JEWELRY

A necklace or bracelet with the image of someone close at heart makes a treasured keepsake. Accent your pieces with letters, photos or other images cut from magazines or scrapbook paper for truly one-of-a-kind creations.

MATERIALS

Bezel pendant blank with chain, or bracelet blank
Desired number of photos or other images
Laminate or clear packing tape
Dry scrapbook adhesive
UV curing resin (such as Magic-Glos)
Toothpicks
Lighter or matches
UV lamp, direct sunlight or a fluorescent black light in a desk lamp

DIRECTIONS

1. Cut photo or photos to fit inside pendant or bracelet blank. For bracelet, cut all pieces needed to fill entire length.
2. Use laminate or clear packing tape to cover each photo (this protects the colors in the photos from the resin). Trim any excess laminate or tape so it is flush with the edges of photo.
3. Affix each photo in desired blank with a dab of dry scrapbook adhesive. (Do not use liquid or tacky glue, which may not dry completely under the resin.) Press firmly into place.
4. Following the resin manufacturer's instructions, fill the indented bezel area on top of each photo with resin, spreading it evenly with a toothpick. If bubbles form, gently and carefully wave a lit match or lighter over them.
5. Harden the resin by placing it in direct sunlight or under a UV lamp for 20-60 minutes, following the resin manufacturer's suggestions for time. (Do not touch to see if resin is dry because fingerprints will mar it.)
6. When resin has hardened, place the pendant on chain.

MIXED MEDIA CHOKER NECKLACE

Create a pretty, romantic necklace using simple techniques and only a few materials, including ribbon trim, beads and cording.

MATERIALS

Gathered or pleated ribbon trim
Cord (faux metallic leather, suede or simple cord)
Choice of 6 large beads (3 sets of 2 matching beads)
Choice of 6 bead caps
Toggle clasp
Round clasp (to attach to flower back)
Hot glue gun

Needle and coordinating colored thread

DIRECTIONS

1. Starting at end of ribbon trim, fold over edge and wrap length of ribbon in a circular motion around itself to create a flower design. Hot-glue inside back edge while wrapping. Layer loosely for a full flower shape. When the flower is the desired size, trim end, fold over the edge and adhere in place with hot glue.

2. Use needle and coordinating colored thread to attach round clasp centered on the back of the flower. Secure clasp on 2 sides, allowing space to thread the cord through.

3. Determine length of necklace based on recipient's neck size. Cording will need to be doubled and also be longer than final necklace length (tying knots will decrease the total length).

4. Thread cord through one half of the toggle clasp. Fold cord in half, with the clasp at the fold and the cord ends meeting, to create a double-stranded necklace. Tie a knot at clasp base to secure cord in place. (At this point, confirm that the double-stranded necklace is approximately 1½ times longer than needed for neck size.)

5. Tie a second knot about 4 in. from clasp. Thread a series of 3 beads and 3 bead caps onto the double-strand cord as seen in photo. Gather beads and caps snugly against one another. Tie a knot to secure all in place.

6. About 1 in. from the knot, thread the flower onto the double-strand cord. To secure flower, use needle and thread or hot glue on back near the round clasp.

7. About 1 in. from the flower, tie another knot. Add beads and bead caps in the same order as on the first side of the necklace to create a symmetrical design. Gather the beads and caps snugly against each another. Tie a knot to secure all in place.

8. About 4 in. from knot, thread both cords through the second half of the toggle clasp. (Be sure both sides of the necklace have symmetrical spacing between knots.) Tie a double knot to secure the cord to the clasp; trim any excess cord.

> ### HOMEMADE HELPER
> When choosing cord, beads and bead caps, be sure the holes are large enough to accommodate two strands of cord.

wrapped wire in place with your fingers as you go.

4. To secure the wrapped wire, thread the end of the wrapped wire between two beads from the bottom to the top and pull tight. Thread wire a few more times between the same two beads in the same way. Repeat between the next two beads and continue until you have secured the wire in all three gaps between the beads.

5. Repeat steps 3 and 4, wrapping the wire around the perimeter 8-10 times and then securing the wire between the bead gaps.

6. Wrap the remaining 6-in. end of wire a few times through the center back of the nest, then wrap it a few times over either the base of a pin back or the end of a kilt pin, securing it on the back of the nest. Wrap wire again through the center back of the nest a few times.

7. Use needle-nose or round-nose pliers to create coils in the remaining ends of wire on the top of nest. Use wire cutters to trim off excess wire.

WIRE BIRD'S NEST BROOCH

Let creativity take wing with an adorable gift for the bird lovers you know. Small blue beads form the eggs in the little wire nest, which makes a distinctive accessory when you attach a pin back or kilt pin.

MATERIALS
6-ft. length of 20-gauge wire
Three 8-mm round blue beads or pearls
¾-in. pin back or 2-in. kilt pin
Wire cutters
Needle-nose pliers
Round-nose pliers
Wood pencil or ¼-in. dowel rod

DIRECTIONS
1. For the eggs, string the beads or pearls onto the wire, placing them together about 6 in. from one end of the wire. Bend the wire so that the beads form a triangular cluster. Secure the beads in place by twisting the wires together a few times where they meet.

2. Wrap the long end of the wire around the length of the pencil or dowel rod, creating a spiraled wire. Pull the wire out to create loose waves along the length of the wire.

3. Beginning at the twisted area by the beads, wrap the long wavy wire around the perimeter of the bead cluster 8-10 times, wrapping loosely and holding the

STAMPED CLAY EARRINGS

Your girlfriends will love these unique earrings made from moldable polymer clay. Use a rubber-stamp to easily create the designs. Have a little bit of extra time? Create a matching pendant.

MATERIALS
Polymer clay
Desired rubber stamp
Small piece of Plexiglas or other hard, flat surface
Foil-lined baking sheet
Waxed paper
Acrylic paint in desired color
Sponge brush
Paper towels
Toothpick
2 earring wires
Two 3-mm closed jump rings
Two 7-mm open jump rings
Ultrafine sandpaper
Long-nose pliers
Standard oven

DIRECTIONS
1. Condition the clay by rolling and kneading it in your hands until it is pliable.
2. Make 2 same-size balls of clay and shape each into a slight cylinder.
3. Lay the clay cylinders on a piece of waxed paper. Use Plexiglas or other surface to flatten the cylinders into same-size ovals.
4. Press the rubber stamp in the clay, making a similar impression on both clay ovals.
5. With toothpick, make a hole at the top of each oval.
6. Place the ovals on a foil-lined baking sheet and bake in the oven following the clay manufacturer's instructions. Let cool.
7. Use a sponge brush to apply paint on the stamped pattern. Wipe off excess paint with a paper towel, leaving paint only in the stamped impression. Let dry.
8. Lightly sand top of each bead to remove any remaining paint that is outside the impression. Buff with paper towel. Place the beads back in oven at the manufacturer's recommended temperature for 10 minutes to set the paint. Let cool.
9. Use pliers to open 7-mm jump ring by carefully twisting ends sideways. (Do not pull apart.) Slip open jump ring through the hole on an oval. Slide on 3-mm jump ring. Use pliers to close larger jump ring. Add jump rings to remaining oval in the same way.
10. Use pliers to open the hoop of an earring wire. Slip 3-mm jump ring onto it and close hoop. Add earring wire to remaining earring in same way.

Pretty
PAPER
CRAFTS

FOLDED PAPER CANDY BOXES

Create simple candy gift boxes by following the templates and folding card stock. The boxes look impressive, yet they're so easy to make!

MATERIALS

Printed enlarged box and angel wings templates (below)
Patterned card stock (or heavy scrapbook paper)
Ribbon or pipe cleaners
Pompoms or any desired embellishments
Painter's tape (or low adhesive tape)
Craft knife with cutting mat
Hole punch
Hot glue gun

NOTE: When selecting embellishments, keep in mind that one side of the box will open. Avoid attaching anything that would block the box from being opened.

BOX (EACH)

1. Following the outside lines, cut out the printed enlarged box template. Place the template on back of card stock; secure with tape. Use a craft knife with cutting mat or scissors to cut around the outer edge of the template. Remove the tape and template from the cutout.

2. Using a ruler as a guide, mark the score lines with a soft pencil. Use the craft knife to gently score the marked lines. Punch two small holes on opposite sides of the design (shown on template).

3. Fold over the tabbed edges and fold up the sides to create a pyramid shape. Carefully apply hot glue to the folded tabs, one side at a time. Leave one of the sides of the box (a side with a hole punched in it) open.

4. Fill the box with wrapped candy or snacks or a small toy. Once the box is full, close it gently, making sure the tabs are folded in. Thread the ribbon or pipe cleaner through the punched holes, going in through the assembled side of the box first and out through the open wall. Tie the ribbon or twist the pipe cleaner to secure tightly.

ANGEL EMBELLISHMENT

Use the enlarged, copied template to cut out angel wings. (If paper is not a double-sided design, cut out 2 opposite template pieces and glue them together with the design sides facing out). With a craft knife, gently score lines as indicated on template. Apply hot glue to the space between the score lines and adhere the wings to the back of the box (opposite the open side). Use gold pipe cleaner to create the angel's head and halo.

OTHER EMBELLISHMENTS

Embellish boxes as desired or follow the examples in the photo. Use a pompom or cotton for the top of Santa's hat; make the fuzzy hat trim by cutting up pompoms and adhering the pieces to the box. Use a gold star as the top of the Christmas tree.

FOLDED PAPER CANDY BOXES PATTERNS

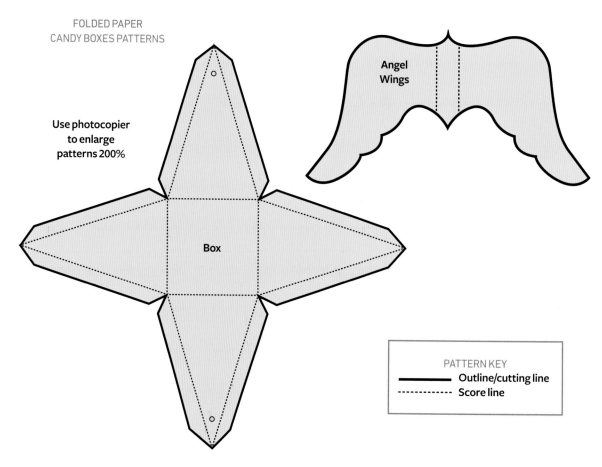

Use photocopier to enlarge patterns 200%

Angel Wings

Box

PATTERN KEY
—— Outline/cutting line
- - - - - Score line

JAPANESE FOUR-HOLE BOUND BOOKS

A traditional Japanese binding technique is the secret behind these beautiful books. Best of all, you are likely to have many of the materials this project calls for on hand.

MATERIALS (FOR ONE)

10 sheets of plain standard-size copy paper, cut in half crosswise
2 sheets of 5½x8½-in. decorative paper for covers
Waxed linen thread, embroidery floss or twine
Binder clip
Large-eye long needle (such as a sail needle or upholsterer's pin)
Thumbtack or awl
Craft knife
Self-healing cutting mat

NOTE: When sewing, keep the thread taut and neat around the spine.

MAKING THE PAGES

1. Set aside 1 piece of copy paper to use for template.
2. Lay 1 decorative sheet of paper, right side down, on work surface. Stack the remaining copy paper pages on top. Place remaining decorative sheet, right side up, on top of stack.
3. On template paper, draw a line 1 in. from a short edge. Fold template in half lengthwise 3 times and unfold.
4. Draw dots along the line at the intersections of the first, third, fifth and seventh creases. With the template right side up and the dots on the left, label the dots 1, 2, 3 and 4, starting from bottom.
5. Place template on top of the stack. Hold everything together with a binder clip opposite the dotted side.
6. On cutting mat, press a thumbtack or awl through each dot. Flip book and press again through the holes to widen. With book stack right side up, use a pencil to lightly label the holes 1, 2, 3 and 4 the same as for the template.

SEWING THE SPINE

1. Cut a length of thread measuring about 33 in. and thread the needle.
2. With stacked paper right side up, bring needle up from the back of book through hole 2, leaving a 2- to 3-in. tail at back. Wrap thread around spine and bring thread up through hole 2.
3. Bring thread through hole 1. Wrap the thread around the spine and bring back through hole 1. Wrap around book base and bring back down through hole 1.
4. Bring thread up through hole 2 and back down through hole 3.

5. Bring thread up through hole 4. Wrap thread around spine and bring back up through hole 4. Wrap thread around head of book and bring back up through hole 4.
6. Bring thread through hole 3. Wrap thread around spine and bring back down through hole 3.
7. Bring thread up through hole 2. On front, loop thread around cross-stitch between holes 1 and 2.
8. Bring thread down through hole 2. Cut the thread; tie ends with a double knot at back of book near hole 2. Trim ends.

BLOCK-PRINTED CARDS

A handwritten note on a handmade card? How charming! Use the block-print technique, and experiment with designs and colors.

MATERIALS

Tracing paper
Card stock or decorative paper and envelopes
Block printing ink (water soluble)
Linoleum or other printing block (such as Soft-Kut or Speedy-Carve)
Linoleum cutting tools in various sizes
Rigid plastic sheet for rolling surface
Palette knife
Brayer (rolling tool)
Block printing baren, optional

CARVING BLOCK

1. Draw a simple design freehand or choose a shape from a child's book or other source. Using a soft pencil, trace desired design onto tracing paper. Lay traced design face down onto printing block. Transfer design by rubbing the back of paper with a spoon, making sure image doesn't shift.

2. Decide where you want ink to show in the print (carved areas will not hold ink). Carve out desired areas using linoleum cutting tools, carving away from you for safety.

3. When carved design is complete, use cutting tool with a large blade to cut the outer edge from block. Clear shavings. If needed, run block under lukewarm water and pat dry.

4. Place a dollop of ink on plastic sheet and even out ink with palette knife. With light pressure, use brayer to roll the ink in several directions. When the ink begins to resemble the texture of an orange peel, roll the brayer in a single direction to coat the roller.

5. With the block design face up on your work surface, roll inked brayer in one direction over block to cover the design.

PRINTING CARDS

1. If the block is large or the carved design is intricate, keep the block ink side up on work surface, lay a piece of test paper or card stock on top of block and use the baren to exert even pressure on the paper for a uniform impression. If the block is small and looks more like a stamp, firmly press the block ink side down onto test paper or card stock, being careful not to shift the block.

2. Inspect the test design. If needed, carve out additional areas on block or add more ink, then test again.

3. When satisfied with design, block-print desired paper or card stock. Let dry. Fold paper or card stock to form cards.

> ### HOMEMADE HELPER
> If your craft store does not carry all the supplies for this project, look for them at art supply stores.

PAPER ORNAMENT GIFT TAGS

This year, add a personal touch to your wrapped gifts. Create cute ornament-shaped tags using decorative scrapbook paper, card stock or whatever paper you might have on hand.

MATERIALS

Ornament patterns (at far right)
Tracing paper
Scrapbook paper or card stock in assorted solid colors and patterns
Coordinating narrow ribbon
Craft glue

DIRECTIONS

1. Trace ornament patterns onto tracing paper and cut out.
2. Trace each pattern onto the back of 2 coordinating sheets of scrapbook paper or card stock. Cut out shapes.
3. For each ornament, choose one of the 2 cutouts to be used as the background piece. Cut the remaining shape horizontally in half or in 3 pieces. Glue 1 or 2 pieces to the background piece so that part of the background remains visible, aligning the outer edges. Let dry completely.
4. On each ornament, glue a short length of ribbon horizontally across the edges where the different paper pieces meet, concealing the edges. Let dry. Trim the ribbon even with the outer edges of ornaments.
5. Cut a short length of ribbon for each ornament. Glue it in a loop at the top of each ornament.
6. Write on back or front of tags as desired, and attach to packages.

> **HOMEMADE HELPER**
> Embellish the gift tags with miniature jingle bells, additional ribbon or scrapbooking accessories.

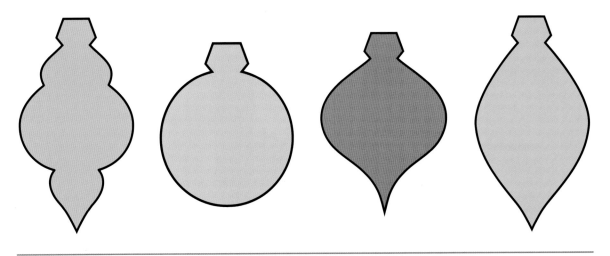

BLANK NOTECARDS

Give **old cards** new life as brand-new greetings. Using a set of **craft punches**, cut out phrases and shapes and adhere to **blank cards** with **craft glue**. Accessorize with **scrapbooking letters** and **washi tape**.

BUTTON CARDS

Upcycle **this year's cards** into next year's by cutting out your favorite images and messages with **scissors**. Arrange on **blank cards** and embellish with **buttons, ribbon, twine, doilies** and **washi tape**. Adhere details with **craft glue** or, for heavier items such as buttons, **hot glue**.

REPEATING LOOP

Layers of curls stack up to become a pretty package topper.

MATERIALS

Spool of 1½-in.-wide ribbon
Hot glue gun
Scissors

DIRECTIONS

1. Pull a piece of ribbon from the spool about one-third longer than the desired length of the final bow. Do not cut the ribbon from the spool yet. Lay the ribbon on a work surface with the loose end on the left and the spool on the right.
2. Loop the left side back onto itself halfway to create the bottom left-hand loop of the bow. Hot-glue the end down.
3. Pull more ribbon from the spool and loop over the entire bow length, stopping just short of the left side. Glue that layer down in the center to make the bottom right-hand loop. Double the ribbon back over the left side to start the second layer, gluing in the center to secure.
4. Continue looping and gluing until the bow is as full as desired; cut ribbon. Cut a 4-inch-long piece of ribbon from the spool. Loop that piece around the center of the bow to hide the folds; secure on the back with hot glue.

SHINING STAR

Make this three-dimensional ornament to hang on doorknobs or cabinet pulls.

Using the template below, cut 10 star points from **old Christmas cards** using a **craft knife** and a **ruler** to keep the edges straight.

Lightly score each point vertically down the center on the back. Fold each along the score line. Lay 5 points in a star shape and **tape** together on the back. Repeat with remaining 5 points.

Place the 2 stars together and tape on the inside. Coat the edges with **glitter glue** and dry thoroughly.

Thread a **needle** with a **thin ribbon** and punch it through a star tip to create a hanging loop.

Enlarge template 210% to make a 9-in. star.

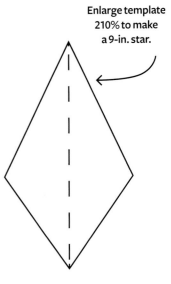

DIY GIFT WRAP

Give Christmas gifts a charming handmade touch with your own wrap made with kraft paper and paint. Have fun using a variety of household items as stamps.

MATERIALS

Kraft paper roll
Items to be used for stamping
(cushioning wrap, corrugated
cardboard, a pencil eraser, a
wine bottle cork, rubber bands
and a small wood block)
Craft paints of choice
Paint palette or cardboard
Foam pouncers
Large and small craft knives
Cutting mat

STAMPS

1. For Christmas trees, use the large craft knife to cut triangles of varying sizes from corrugated cardboard.
2. For snowflakes, use the small craft knife to cut 4 small triangles from the top of wine cork, evenly spacing them around cork to create a snowflake shape on top of cork.
3. For a graphic line design, wrap the small wood block with desired number of rubber bands.

GIFT WRAP

1. Spread craft paint of desired color on palette or piece of cardboard.
2. Using foam pouncer, apply paint to the desired stamp, being careful to coat only the raised areas of the design with paint.
3. Firmly press stamp onto the kraft paper and lift. Continue stamping to cover the desired amount of paper roll.
4. Let wrapping paper dry completely before using.

HOMEMADE HELPER

Many ordinary household items may be used as stamps for this project. Feel free to experiment with any on-hand items you like. Practice stamping on scrap paper or cardboard to master the technique before stamping on kraft paper.

SCRAPPY, SPARKLY ORNAMENTS

Shred **cards** and leftover **sparkly gift wrap**. Fill a **transparent ornament ball** with the pieces. Loop a **coordinating ribbon** through ornament top and hang on the tree.

HOLIDAY WINE BOTTLE LABELS

Whether you're giving wine as a gift or setting up a buffet, make a label that matches the occasion. Personalize the labels with a photo if you'd like.

MATERIALS

Assorted scrapbook paper or card stock, 8x10 in.
Assorted scrapbook paper pieces, 3x5 in. or smaller
Double-sided tape
Tulle
Ribbon
Twine
Hole punch
Rubber stamp and stamp pad
Scrapbook three-dimensional stickers or tags of choice

DIRECTIONS

1. Choose a scrapbook paper or card stock and cut it into a 10x4-in. strip. This strip should fit around a standard wine bottle and will be the base of the label.

2. Choose a smaller scrapbook paper to layer on the base label. Run double-sided tape from corner to corner on the back of the smaller piece and adhere them to the base label. Layer colors and shapes of paper until you reach desired design.

3. To add tulle, cut a 6-in. piece of tulle. Bunch tulle lengthwise and wrap around the label top to bottom. Secure each end with double-sided tape on the back of the label.

4. To add a ribbon that you can also use to tie the label in the back, center a length of ribbon on the label, lined up so that the ends of ribbon are even once around the back of the bottle. Run double-sided tape on the back of ribbon where it touches the label and adhere it to the label.

5. To finish the label, add scrapbook stickers to the front of the label.

6. Add a tag with twine or double-sided tape. Or, if you added tulle in step 3, make a hole in the tulle with a hole punch, thread string or twine through the hole, and tie on a card or a paper tag.

NOTE: If using card stock, form it around the bottle before using double-sided tape so that the seal will hold.

INDEX